Express Publis

by Karl Dunkerley

ISBN 07457 0220 1

Kuma

Express Publisher Illustrated

©1992 Karl Dunkerley

Published by:

Kuma Computers Ltd
12 Horseshoe Park
Pangbourne
Berks
RG8 7JW

Tel 0734 844335
Fax 0734 844339

Other Computing Titles From Kuma:

IBM PC & Compatible Micros

DTP Sourcebook - Fonts & Clip Art for the PC by J. L. Borman	07457 0030 6
PageMaker 4.0 for Windows by William B. Sanders	07457 0031 4
ZBasic Quick Reference Guide for PC & Mac by John Sumner	07457 0140 X
The Windows Guide Book by Gill Gerhardi, Vic Gerhardi & Andy Berry	07457 0041 1
A Practical Guide to Timeworks Publisher 2 on the PC by Terry Freedman	07457 0147 7
The DR DOS 6 Quick Start Guide by John Sumner	07457 0038 1
Illustrated DR DOS 6 - The First 20 Hours by John Sumner	07457 0044 6
The User's Guide to Money Manager PC by John Sumner	07457 0047 0
Breaking Into Windows 3.1 by Bill Stott & Mark Brearley	07457 0056 X
The Utter Novice Guide to GW Basic by Bill Aitken	07457 0045 4
The Utter Novice Guide to Q Basic by Bill Aitken	07457 0046 2
PagePlus Illustrated by Richard Hunt	07457 0062 4
DOS 5 Quick Start Guide by John Sumner	07457 0054 3

Commodore Amiga

Program Design Techniques for the Amiga by Paul Overaa	07457 0032 2
Intuition A Practical Programmers Guide by Mike Nelson	07457 0143 4
The Little Red Workbench 1.3 Book by Mark Smiddy	07457 0048 9
The Little Blue Workbench 2 Book by Mark Smiddy	07457 0055 1

Apple Macintosh

DTP Sourcebook - Fonts & Clip Art for the Mac by J. L. Borman	07457 0050 0
ZBasic Quick Reference Guide for PC & Mac by John Sumner	07457 0140 X
The Quark Book by Rod Lawton & Isaac Davis	07457 0052 7

Psion Organiser

Psion Organiser Deciphered by Gill Gerhardi, Vic Gerhardi & Andy Berry	07457 0139 6
Using & Programming the Psion Organiser by Mike Shaw	07457 0134 5
File Handling on the Psion Organiser by Mike Shaw	07457 0135 3
Machine Code Programming on the Psion Organiser 2nd Ed. by Bill Aitken	07457 0138 8
Psion Organiser Comms Handbook by Gill & Vic Gerhardi & Andy Berry	07457 0154 X

Psion Series 3

First Steps in Programming the Psion Series 3 by Mike Shaw	07457 0145 0
Serious Programming on the Psion Series 3 by Bill Aitken	07457 0035 7

Atari ST

Atari ST Explored 2nd Ed. by John Braga & Malcolm McMahon	07457 0141 8
Program Design Techniques for the Atari ST by Paul Overaa	07457 0029 2
Programming by Example - ST Basic by Dr. G. McMaster	07457 0142 6
A Practical Guide to Calamus Desktop Publishing by Terry Freedman	07457 0159 0
A Practical Guide to Timeworks on the Atari ST by Terry Freedman	07457 0158 2

Cambridge Z88

Z88 Magic by Gill Gerhardi, Vic Gerhardi & Andy Berry	07457 0137 X

Games

Sega Megadrive Secrets by Rusel deMaria	07457 0037 3
Sega Megadrive Secrets Volume 2 by Rusel deMaria	07457 0043 8
Corish's Computer Games Guide	07457 0150 7
Awesome Sega Megadrive Secrets	07457 0226 0

Sharp IQ 7000 & 8000

Using Basic on the Sharp IQ by John Sumner	07457 0034 9

A selection from our fast-expanding range - latest full details on request

A Guide to Desktop Publishing
by Terry Freedman

The aim of the book is to explain the basic principles of Desktop Publishing (DTP) including how to achieve certain effects, what sort of things to avoid (e.g. 'fontmania') and the sort of features to look for in a DTP program.

The book is targeted to new DTP users and those considering buying a DTP package.

Contents:

What is DTP	Header	Resolution
What can you do with a DTP package?	Footer	Raster Settings
	Group	
DTP, word processors and document processors	Frame Handling	Useful Hardware
	Sizing	Introduction
Do you need DTP?	Proportionate Sizing	RAM explained
	Positioning	Storage media & capacity
The DTP Process	Moving	Computer Power
The Design Brief	Copying	Monitor Types
From Idea to finished product:	Real Copies	Mouse
stages	Virtual Copies	Printer
	Deleting	Scanner
How DTP packages work:	Pasting	Flatbed
Basic Principles	Selecting	Handheld
Frames	Grouping	OCR
Style Sheets/Layout	Ungrouping	Video Digitiser
Master Pages/Saved Pages/Templates	Stacking	
		Useful software
Importing and Exporting	Features	Word Processor (minimum features needed)
•	Columns	
Preparing text for DTP	Graphics	Art package
ASCII	Graphics & text flows	Clip Art
	Font Size	
Preparing Artwork	Font Style	Dos and Don'ts
Scanning	Autoflow	Widows
Video Digitising	Add/insert pages	orphans
Painting/drawing packages	Move pages	White Space
Vector Graphics	Delete Pages	Fontmania
Bitmapped Graphics	Save Pages	Drop-shadow Disease
		Boxes
Frame Types	About printing	
Text	Types of printer	Principle of Layout
rotated Text	Dot matrix family	Ideas for Layouts
Vector Graphics	Inkjet family	
Bitmapped Graphics	Laser	

Price £12.95

ISBN 07457 0039 X

Contents

Starting Desk Top Publishing
with Express Publisher v2.0 for DOS

1.	ReadMe First	1
2.	Terms and Useful Tips	13
3.	Introducing Desk Top Publishing	49
4.	Devising a Value-For-Money D.T.P. System	59
5.	Setting Up Express Publisher for Dos v2.0	79

The Nuts and Bolts of Express Publisher

6.	Starting Express Publisher	91
7.	Handling Text	99
8.	Handling Graphics	127
9.	The 'TextEffect' Package	151

Developing Complete Publications

10.	Mixing Text, TextEffect and Graphics	163
11.	Creating a Complete Publication	177
12.	Printing Publications	199
13.	Designing Your own Publication	205

Memory Size

DTP Documents use a lot of the computer's memory. Therefore you may have problems if your documents are large and your memory is limited. This is like trying to turn an elephant around in a small cage. A lot of manoeuvring is needed tor the desired result is achieved.

Again, straightforward actions may seem to pause for ages. You may even feel that your computer has 'hung' (doing nothing) or 'crashed' (gone mad). Often this will be due to a lack of memory. Just sit tight and buy a percolator. Coffee Factor 10.

However, do not act rashly and switch the machine off. If you find certain actions do cause problems, it is a good idea to save the document in its current state before starting this action. It hanging or crashing do occur then at least you do not hav-e to start the document from scratch.

Hard Disk Capacity

Although DTP can be used without a hard-disk, it is virtually unworkable. Forget it. Documents tend to take up a lot of disk space. The bigger capacity the disk (measured in 'megabytes') the better for two reasons. The first is that on a small disk, saving can be painfully slow. This is because EPDos is looking for room to save parts of the document.

Like a small car park, small disk is more likely to be crowded (most of the parking spaces have gone). You have to drive around to find a suitable spot. The bigger the disk, the more spots available and the lower the Coffee Factor. If saving is slow or seems to hang then this is the likely problem.

The second problem is that if memory is limited and the document big, EPDos will put less heavily-used part of the document onto disk as a temporary measure. It can then concentrate on the task in hand. However, when you move to another part of the document, it brings this off the disk and into memory. The smaller the disk, the longer this takes for the reasons given above. Coffee Factor up.

B2. Software Setup

Memory Handling

It is not only the physical hardware that can affect EPDos's performance. A PC relies on a program known as a 'DOS' (or Disk Operating System) in order to function properly. Different companies have produced different versions although each should run the same programs.

However, some handle memory better than others. The better ones help programs run faster and crash less often. The latest generation is usually the best. For Microsoft's Dos this is version 5.0 and for Digital Research it is version 6.0. Do not use an earlier version than v3.0 of either

If you experience crashing or hanging on several different programs then this may be the cause. Upgrading the DOS can improve matters greatly.

Text Effect

TextEffect is a program within a program (EPDos) that greatly extends the range of features available. It has been done in this way so as to save on the total amount of memory needed to run properly.

TextEffect allows you to create much catchier and flashier headlines and logos than from within the main program. When you switch from EPDos to TextEffect, the current document is saved temporarily. Therefore, the more memory and disk space you have the faster this switching will be.

Pop-Up programs

This is the popular name for a type of program that sits in the computer's memory until called up using a special sequence of keystrokes. They are also called 'Terminate and Stay Resident programs (or T.S.R.s).

For example, a pop-up clock program may load each time you start the computer. When you need to know the time you may have to press the keys marked 'Esc' and 'Fl' simultaneously. The time then appears on the screen. To remove this you normally press the same keys again.

Pop-ups are generally utility programs not included in normal programs. They can be very useful indeed. However, they are not wiped out or deleted when you have finished using them. As the long-winded name suggests, they terminate and stay resident in the system.

They are using memory to do this which may be required by EPDos. This can slow it down at times. Coffee consumption increases. Sometimes, a pop-up can result in EPDos behaving strangely.

If your system has pop-ups and you experience crashing or hanging regularly, and there is no other obvious cause, you may need to remove the pop-up completely. It is best not to run the pop-up in the first place if possible. If the problem persists then the pop-up(s) are not the problem.

C. What This Book Aims To Do

C1. How to Use D.T.P.

This book will show you how to use EPDos's features. However, it also aims to show you how to use DTP properly. Many of the principles you learning from this book will be valid when transferring to other packages and even other forms of publishing.

For example, you may want to use EPDos for all general needs such as advertising flyers or handbills. With a basic set-up you should achieve perfectly acceptable results.

Later on, though, you may need a much higher quality of design and printing. The knowledge you will gain from this book will help you communicate more effectively when talking to publishing professionals. It will make it easier to get what you want.

C2. Putting a D.T.P. System Together

Having decided that you need a DTP system, you need to decide what kind of system you want. If you have little knowledge of computing then it is probably best to buy a ready-made system from a high street retailer.

If you know something about computers then you can buy from a much wider range of sources such as mail-order and direct-import.

This book will help you decide what kind of system is best for your needs and where to buy from.

C3. Learning the Basics of EPDos

The main aim of EPI is to teach you to use the EPDos package's many features. The exercises are designed to help you build up skills in using each feature before embarking on complete projects.

This should help readers who are 'feeling' their way around DTP and computing. It should also help you understand the way DTP works much better.

For example, EPDos has facilities for drawing rectangles, circles and lines. Each is shown in turn before you are shown how to combine these features to draw simple pictures. Later in the book, you are shown more advanced uses when compiling more extensive documents.

C4. Putting the Basics Together

When you have learnt several topics (each covering several features), you are shown how to put these together to create a design. For example, when you have learnt about text and graphics as separate topics, you are shown how to combine these.

C5. Designing Your Documents

One of the fallacies of DTP is that it is easy. Many books simply show you how to use a particular DTP package's features. EPI goes beyond this by showing you easy ways to decide on document design. This is often the hardest part of the process once you have learnt the basics.

An important maxim in computing has always been, 'Do not re-invent the wheel'. In other words, if someone else has done something similar to what you want, study it and learn from it.

The message of this book is that even beginners can produce good documents even without taking a course in design.

D. The Format of 'Express Publisher Illustrated'

D 1. The Sections

The first section is designed to give you the basic knowledge about what DTP is all about and putting together a complete and workable system without busting the budget.

The second will teach you how to use all the features contained within EPDos. This contains all the exercises that will help you compile documents.

The third section is concerned with helping you to create good-looking and effective documents . It shows you how to generates ideas, gives the general rules of layout and type use and where to find other information you might need.

D2. The Chapters

Chapter 2.
A glossary of useful terms used in DTP and computing plus information on the different parts of the screens used in EPDos and TextEffect.

Chapter 3.
Having learnt the lingo, you can then learn about DTP, its history, the uses it can be put to, and the concepts used in publishing in general.

Chapter 4.
For those thinking of investing in their own DTP system, this chapter will help you decide what your needs are, what kind of system fits the bill, and how to go about putting it together. If you have a basic system, ways of improving it are given. The emphasis is on cost-benefit.

Chapter 5.
This will help you set up EPDos on your computer system and sets out the minimum needed. Problems you might encounter and how to deal with them are discussed.

Chapter 6.
Having installed your system, you can now go on a guided tour that will allow you to understand what you see on the screen, how to enter commands and how to start a new document.

Chapter 7.

The first of the skill-learning chapters. This one concerns how to enter text and how to modify it.

Chapter 8.

Having learnt how to use text, it is time to learn the art of graphics, both making up your own and incorporating pictures already available.

Chapter 9.

Demonstrates the facilities contained in the TextEffect package for making headlines, banners, logos, etc.

Chapter 10.

This is where the three previous topics are combine to show you how they interact with one another. The exercises will guide through the creation of a one-page advertising flyer with the stress on catching the eye.

Chapter 11.

The previous chapters showed how to put a multi-page design together. This chapter shows you how to create a complete document and to set up standard layouts ready for the real text and pictures to be entered.

Chapter 12.

Having created your complete document, you need to see it 'in the flesh'. Printing always sounds like a straightforward feature but it often isn't.

Chapter 13.

Design ideas are all around us in this modern age. If you are not a designer then you can often 'crib' basic ideas and modify them for your own needs. Like most things worthwhile, DTP is 1% inspiration and 99% perspiration

D3. The Conventions Used

Press

When you see this symbol, it means that you should press the key indicated to the right. If more than one key is shown then they should be pressed simultaneously or the first held down followed by the others until all are depressed together.

Bottom Line

This means that you should look at the borttom of the screen to see the statement or instructions.

Statement
This is where EPDos is telling you something. Sometimes This is just to inform you of what is happening, other times it is to warn you.

Dialog Box
This warns you that a Dialog Box will appear on screen to ask you questions or warn you. The Dialog Box name (if it has one) will be shown to the right of the symbol.

Type
This symbol means that you need to type the reply or statement shown to its right.

Move Mouse
This means that you must use your mouse to move around the screen or select an object on the page or from a menu list.

Left-Clicking
When you see this symbol, you should click the mouse button indicated by either LC for Left-Button Click or RC for Right-Button Click. This generally has the effect of selecting an object (text or graphic). You may then have to choose the action you want performing on the object and confirm it using a dialog box.

Double-Clicking
If the symbol is repeated, side-by-side, this means you should click the button twice in rapid succession. This usually means that you want to both select an object and confirm the action to be taken without using the dialog box. It can only be used in certain circumstances. Further instruction is given later in the chapter on Starting EPDos.

Chapter 2. Terms and Useful Tips

A. Glossary of Terms

A1. Computing Terms   14
A2. Publishing Terms   25

B. The Express Publisher Screen

B1.   Icons   38
B2. Menus   42
B3. Function Key Short-cuts   44
B4. Text and Dialog Keys   44

C. The TextEffect Screen

C1. Icons   45
C2. Menus   46
C3. Keyboard Short-cuts   47

A. Glossary of Terms

A 1. Computing Terms

Bubble Jet

A Form of Cheap, Quality Printer

A type of page printer that uses a print head containing small nozzles. These nozzles squirt small bubbles of ink that form dots on the page. Some are capable of around 360 dots per inch which gives a good quality of print. Cheap, quiet and compact. Increasingly popular. Ideal for use in the home or the office. An excellent alternative to the noisier, dearer and bulkier laser printer.

C. P. U.

The Heart of the P. C. 's Hardware

Short for Central Processing Unit. This is the heart of a computer. PC-Compatibles can have processors in the Intel series of '86 chips. The first generation was known as the 8086 and followed by the 80286, 80386, and 80486. The '80' is usually ignored, i.e., the 286 etc.

Character Sets Foreign languages and graphical symbols Most keyboards can be used to access characters in foreign languages plus graphical symbols. There are different ways of accessing these alternatives. Some packages allow access from within themselves but otherwise you might need to modify your Dos system.

Clear

Removal of text, pictures or graph

The removal of certain items from a document or the wiping of the whole document. Clearing can be achieved by either selecting an object or text and then pressing the Delete key or by menu selection.

Clicking

Using Mouse Button to Activate /Highlight

The action of pressing a button on the mouse to active a command or select some object. Often clicking once merely highlights rather than activates a command or option. Clicking twice in rapid succession, or 'Double-Clicking' will start an action.

For example, when restarting a document that already exists, the 'Open' command will list all the documents in the current disk directory. Clicking once only highlights the document name. Double-clicking will actually start the document.

14

Colours

Altering the Screen Layout Colours

In Express Publisher for Dos v2.0 this only refers to the colours on the screen display, assuming you have a colour monitor. You can change the colour of the scroll bars, titles and rules.

Copy

Repeating Text or Graphics

You may want to repeat text or graphics elsewhere in a document. This may consist of one or more items which you would prefer not to recreate yourself due to time or complexity. The item is copied to a reserved area of computer memory until you decide where to insert or *Paste* it. The original remains intact and in position

Cutting

Removing or Moving Text or Graphics

Items no longer needed in the document can be cut out. In reality, the text is not lost immediately but stored in a reserved area of computer memory until something else is cut or copied.

Thus, the item can be moved by cutting it and then Pasteing it elsewhere. Used normally when transferring an item to another page.

D.O.S.

Software Controlling the P.C.'s Functions

Stands for Disk Operating System. For P.C.s, this is often referred to as Ms-Dos or PC-Dos. Dos is not a program in the normal sense. It instructs the computer's hardware on how to act. For example, the way data is stored on a disk is determined by Dos. The same is true of the keyboard and many other computer components.

Daisy-Wheel

An Up-market Typewriter-style Printer

Once very popular, especially as computers replaced typewriters on secretaries' desks. A plastic wheel with spokes containing letters and symbols whizzed around very fast until a hammer struck the correct spoke. Similar to the Golfball printer.

Similar to a classy typewriter in quality but very noisy, slow and inflexible. They were ideal for letters as the print was highly professional but had no capacity for printing graphics. Therefore, completely useless for Desk Top Publishing purposes.

Defaults

The Normal Settings of a System

When a system such as a DTP package or printer are set up, they have 'Defaults' set that define how the system operates. For example, your printer will usually be set to print on a tall page rather than a wide one. This Portrait mode is considered the default. If you change the system and then 'reset' this is the setting that will be used.

Delete

The Removal of an Item

If an item is no longer or has been wrongly defined, it may be deleted or removed from the document. The removal can either be permanent or temporary depending on the method used. Removing items is sometimes called Cutting items or objects.

D. T. P.

Desk Top Publishing

The combination of text, pictures, drawings to create reports, documents, advertising, newsletters, papers and magazines. The transfer of traditional publishing methods onto the micro-computer.

Dialog

Communicating with EPDos

When you choose a command from one of the menus, you may find a Dialog Box opening up. This will contain information you need, the state of various items and the space to enter commands. For example, to print out a ten-page document, you will choose the Print command from the menu. The Print Dialog Box will open telling you the state of the printer, allowing you to change some items such as the number of pages to be printed.

Directories

The Structure of a Disk

Any disk needs organisation. If a hard disk consisted simply of a disorganised list of files, it would be impossible for users to keep track of work. Consequently, you can group related files together. It is like having an address book. You list all your friends and contacts under the first initial of their surnames. Similarly, all EPDos's files are kept in a directory called Express which has Sub-directories called Art, Docs, etc.

Display Settings

Defines What Objects Shown On Screen

Different types of graphic image can be selected for display on screen. Choices made have an effect on the speed and memory requirements of EPDos. Some items are best displayed in low-resolution to raise speed and lower memory needs. Items printed properly on paper.

Dot Matrix

A Popular Form of Low-Cost Printer

Uses a line of pins which are moved electro-magnetically. This presses into an ink-soaked ribbon to print the dots on paper. The print-head moves across the page to form individual letters or parts of graphics. Dot-matrices may have 9, 18 or 24 pins. However, even the best are essentially low-resolution and low-quality.

Dragging

The Selection and Movement of an Item

DTP gives the user a tremendous freedom to place text and graphics anywhere on a page. For fine and coarse placement, the user can select an item and then move it on the page. This is often called Dragging. The release of the object into the desired place is called *Placing*.

Driver

A Conversion Program for Peripherals

Many computer peripherals, such as printers, conform to different standards and operate in different ways. EPDos users can define which peripheral they use and the relevant Driver will be loaded into the main program when it is run. This converts the document into a format the printer etc. can understand. The better the driver, the more the final output reflects the screen image.

Dropping

Placing an Item in Position on a Page

When an item has been selected and moved on a page, it is placed into position by dropping it. Usually this means releasing the mouse button used to do the movement.

Extensions

Part of a Filename Indicating File Type

Different programs store information on a disk in different Formats. So that users and programs know what type of file is held on the disk, a three-letter extension after the Filename is used to indicate it. For example, 'picture1.bmp' is an image stored in Bitmap format.

Filenames

A Unique Name for a Disk File

On a P.C., information is stored in files on disks. These can have names up to eight characters long plus an *Extension*. Files should generally have unique names to stop confusion and loss of files or data.

However, files kept in different *Directories* can have the same name as the directory should indicate the type of data held. Careful thought should be given to how files are named when there are many in a directory. Consistency is important for later on.

Floppy Disk

The Standard Form of P. C. Storage.

A floppy disk is a form of magnetic storage used to hold both programs and data. They come in a variety of sizes and formats, the two most common being 5.25" and 3.5".

They revolve inside a Drive unit that uses electro-magnetic pulses to change the state of the coating of metal particles. These signals are coded messages that can later be re-interpreted by the computer when retrieving information from the disk.

Formats

The Way Data is Stored or Handled

Different types of information are stored in different ways. Graphics and text are major examples. For reasons of accuracy, speed and compactness, the data is stored on a disk by different methods. The Extension to the filename indicates the format type.

G. U. I.

Graphical User Interface.

This is the means of conveying information on a computer by using pictures and graphics rather than text. Input of direct is more natural where image is important.

For example, to draw a box, a GUI program would let you select an item depicting a box and then use a device such as a Mouse to size and place it. A text-based program would expect you to type in size and co-ordinates. Using and learning GUI programs is usually much faster and friendlier The desired result is easier to achieve.

Grouping

Putting Items Together

Sometimes you will want to carry out the same action on more than one item or object at once. As an example, a piece of text which is linked to a picture may want moving two inches to the left on a page. To ensure they move together precisely, you can select them both before moving and positioning.

Hard Disk

Most Important Form of Storage

Most powerful computer packages would not run without this form of electro-magnetic storage. Its capacity is large by comparison with the standard Floppy Disk and it is much faster. They are measured in Megabytes (one million bytes). If the information stored was in text format, this would equate to one million characters. For personal use, the normal size of a hard disk is between 20 and 100 MByte though they can be far larger.

Hardware

The Components of the Computer

The hardware is basically anything you can physically touch and see. The normal hardware list consists of a main computer box, disk storage, keyboard, screen and printer. Many other items are optional

Importing

Information from one Package to Another

Different programs use different formats for storing information. However, most modern ones can at least read and use information from other packages. Some can even save in another program's format. The action of taking in information in a different format and using it is called importing.

This allows DTP programs to use information created in a wide variety of other programs such as word-processors, picture scanners, drawing packages etc. When you import information, a program called a Filter converts it into the main program's normal format. This is like translating a book from French into English

Ink-Jet

A Popular Form of Printer

See Bubble-Jet

Laser Printer

The Preferred Printer for DTP

Laser Printer work like photocopiers and are popular for many reasons. They are very high quality, relatively quiet, of reasonable speed and clean to run. However, they are expensive to buy and run compared to Bubble-jet and Dot-Matrix printer. Still, they arc a must for many small and large concerns as they are robust, reliable and easy-to-operate.

Menu

A Method of Selecting Features

Rather than type in a command to select a feature, menus allow you to select from a list of possibilities. Usually the full list is hidden until the menu is selected. A sub-menu will then appear until you access precisely the item you require. For example, the main menu list will probably have an item called File from which options to Find, Load, Save and Delete can be selected.

Monitor

Fancy Name for a Computer Screen

Computer Screens come in many varieties conforming to different standards in terms of screen size and quality of picture. For DTP, bigger equals better.

Mouse

Important Manipulation Device in DTP

Without a mouse, DTP is incredibly tedious. Your hand rests on the mouse which contains a rubber ball. As you move the mouse around your desk, small sensors detect this movement and translate it into movement on the screen. Usually an arrow-head or other Pointer can be seen on the screen to indicate position.

The buttons on top of the mouse are operated by your fingers and can be Clicked or Double-Clicked to select object and initiate actions. The sensitivity of the mouse movements can be adjusted to suit your preference, i.e., a small hand movement could cause a large movement on screen or vice-versa. A mouse gives very precise control of .screen items and is fast and flexible.

Objects

A Piece of Text or a Graphic

DTP is the combination of items of text or graphics in a document. Each item is called an Object and can be moved, altered, cut, expanded, deleted etc. to suit your needs and achieve the desired result.

Open

Accessing a Disk File

Disk files are like books. They contain useful data or information but are generally kept closed and put away on a shelf. Computer disk files can be taken off the 'shelf and opened so that you and the program look at and use the information contained inside.

P. C.

The World's Most Popular Computer Type

Now over ten years old, the I.B.M. P.C.-Compatible computer far outsells any other kind by up to ten-to-one. P.C. stands for 'Personal Computer' as the aim was to make even business machines seem personal to the user.

There have been four generations of PC so far, each using a more powerful chip than the last. Huge sales volumes and interchangeable parts have made them extremely cheap and affordable.

Paint Program

Software for Drawing Pictures

Paint programs allow you to 'draw' and colour your own pictures on screen. They range from the very basic to the highly professional. Most have features for drawing simple shapes such as boxes and circles as well a free-hand illustration. EPDos has basic drawing facilities but images from specialist packages can be Imported.

Parallel Port   *Standard Printer Connector*

This is like a plug-hole for connecting a standard printer to a PC. Not all printers use a parallel-type connector but most do. It is very fast and reliable which has made it very popular with makers and users.

Pasting   *Taking Items from Memory onto a Page*

Items of text or graphics that have been Cut or Copied to an area of computer memory can later be Pasted into a new position on a page. However, this can only be done with the very last item cut or pasted as this will replace anything earlier.

Port   *Connection between PC and Peripheral*

Your PC communicates with other pieces of equipment via one or more port. Most PCs are set up with two Serial and one Parallel port. The former are generally more flexible and used for a wide variety of equipment whereas the latter is usually restricted to connecting printers.

Processor   *The 'Chip' that Controls a Computer*

See 'C.P.U.'

R.A.M.   *Random Access Memory*

A flexible form of internal computer memory. It can be changed at any time and any information it holds is lost when the computer is switched off. Measured in Kilo-bytes (approx. 1,000 characters of data) or Megabytes (approx. 1 million characters). For DTP, the more the better. A program is transferred from disk storage into RAM in order to run. RAM memory is made up of silicon chips and circuits.

R.O.M.   *Read-Only Memory*

An inflexible form of internal computer memory. Data and instructions are indelibly etched onto silicon circuits at time of manufacture. This is never lost no matter how often you switch on and off. Many of the most important parts of a PC are held on ROM.

Saving   *Putting Data onto a Computer File*

Data or programs can be transferred from your PC's internal memory to Hard or Floppy Disk for either temporary or permanent storage. This process is know as 'Saving'. Only the current state of the data is transferred, usually replacing previous information.

Scanner

Putting Pictures into Computers

Scanners use reflected light to break up a picture into tiny pieces of information. PCs can then read this and reconstruct the picture in memory for saving to disk and incorporation into documents. Light is shone on the image and the amount and colour of the reflection is recorded. Similar to photocopiers in many ways.

Scroll Bars

An Aid to Moving Around Pages

These are either columns or rows at the edge of the computer screen. They indicate whereabouts you are on a page. This is very useful when working in close-up or zoomed mode for fine adjustments. Scroll bars can also used for moving the page up, down and left, right on the screen. This is useful moving to a new position and seeing more of the page.

Selecting

Choosing an Item of Text or Graphics

When you want to perform an action on a particular item or group of items, you need to select them first. This is done by placing the mouse pointer over the desired object and clicking one of the mouse buttons. Then you select the action or feature you require.

Software

Vital Ingredient in Making PCs Useful

Software is another name for programs. Without these, the computer would be little different from any other piece of machinery. However, unlike Hardware, you cannot touch software. To some, this makes software the 'ghost in the machine'.

Basically, software consists of a set of instructions that tell the computer how to behave in a variety of circumstances. A software package will usually consist of many programs that work together and with files of data. The complexity of some software is staggering.

System Unit

The Computer 'Box'

This is the main part of a PC's Hardware. Usually this sits on the desk top but can stand on the floor or even be incorporated into the whole computer as with a portable machine. Standard contents include the 'motherboard' (holding the main chips and circuits), floppy and hard disks, power supply and connectors for other pieces of equipment. Sometimes the screen sits on top.

Toolbox

The Palette of EPDos Features

These are the basic features available in EPDos. Selected by moving the mouse pointer over the icon or picture and clicking the mouse button.

They include the following tools from left to right;

Arrow	Pointer for selecting items
Text Entry	Typing in text
Text Frame	Setting space aside for text
Box	For drawing rectangles
Rounded Box	Drawing rounded rectangles
Ellipse	Drawing circles and ellipses
Line	Drawing straight lines
Set Line	Decide thickness of lines
Fill	Shading drawn items
Link	Running story between frames
Unlink	Cutting 'thread' of a story
Align	Positioning two frames
Equate	Make two objects same size
Text Wrap	Flowing text around pictures
TextEffect	A program for creating logos, headlines, banners etc.

Undo

Removing the Effect of an Action

Occasionally you might do something to an item or object by mistake. For example, you might move a piece of text to the wrong position. Sometimes it is easier to start the action again than to try and correct it directly. The Undo feature allows you to remove the effect of the last action you undertook. If you moved an item it will move it back to its previous position.

View

Looking at a Page From a Distance

In DTP, you can get the best idea of whether a page layout works or not by looking at the whole page on the screen, even if it is small. You can see obvious imbalances and blunders more easily.

However, fine adjustments are often essential. For this, you need to view the page more closely and alter the view. You will only see a small part rather than the whole page.

Often both are used. In full page view, it is easy to move items from one part of a page to another for rough positioning. Zooming in closer allows fine-tuning.

23

W.I.M.P.

Windows, Icons, Mouse, Pull-Down Menu

A form of G.U.I. that uses the above components to simplify the process of running a program. Their popularity is increasing as they make programs easier to use and more 'natural' to understand.

EPDos is a less-sophisticated form of WIMP program that does not, strictly speaking, use Windows but makes good use of the others. Windows are areas of the entire screen set aside to run different programs in whereas EPDos uses the whole screen. It is more of an IMP than a WIMP program!

W.Y.S.I.W.Y.G.

What You See Is What You Get

Often pronounced 'wissywig', this type of program attempts to create an accurate representation of the finished product on the screen.

This is particularly useful in DTP for maintaining control of the work done. All the items on a page can be seen in their proper form and in the correct position. Small screens can blunt this useful effect.

Zooming

Long-distance and Close-up Page Views

The ability to inspect a page close-up or see the whole page on screen at once. See View.

A2. Publishing Terms

Accent **Guide to Pronunciation**

Marks above or below a letter than indicate how it should be pronounced or stressed in speech.

Aligning **Making Text Line Up**

Where text is laid out in columns, it is preferable to ensure that adjacent lines of text match across. If one line of text sits on an imaginary line, then a more pleasing effect is achieved if text lines either side also sit on this line. The result is more professional.

Attributes **Enhancing /Distinguishing Text and Fonts**

Fonts can be improved by adding certain effects or Attributes such as Italics or Bold. It makes the text stand out from the rest although overuse can have a negative effect. Used in moderation, these can improve text.

Baseline **An Imaginary Line for Straightening Text**

Each line of text sits on a Baseline that can run either along the top of the capital letters or proportionally two-thirds above/one-third below. This ensures that the spacing between lines (see Leading) is maintained if the font remains the same.

Blackletter **Mediaeval Script Fonts**

Used to describe fonts that owe a lot to the very fancy and ornate mediaeval scripts.

Bold **An Attribute to Strengthen a Font**

Bold text is a font that has been thickened all around to give a darker and bulkier typeface. It is very effective in stressing words or passages of particular importance.

Boxes **A Square or Rectangular Graphic**

EPDos contains a built-in tool for creating rectangular or square boxes on a page. These are often used as boundaries to text or graphics, especially where there are several close by or on the same page.

Bring To Front **Place an Item on Top of Others**

If you imagine a pile of cards on a table top, this resembles a page with several overlap items. A card can be put on the top of this pile by Bring To Front. This becomes the uppermost card and is seen most strongly.

Bullets
Dots to Improve the Look of a List

A list of items is often improved by adding Bullets at the beginning of each line. These clearly mark out which lines are the beginning of a new item and which are simply continuation items.

Bitmaps
A Simple Computer Graphic or Picture

A graphic can be described as a collection of differently shaded dots just like the ones in newspapers when looked at under a magnifying glass. This is how some pictures are stored. It is simple and straightforward but has drawbacks. Images are difficult to enlarge without looking 'dotty' or shrink without appearing blotchy.

Character Spacing
The Gaps Between Letters etc.

This defines the amount of space between characters in a sentence. Tight spacing brings them closer to each other and reduces the amount of space between. If the spacing is too tight then letters will merge into each other and become a horrible mess. Loose spacing moves them further apart and widens the space. Excessively loose spacing means that it is harder to distinguish the words in a sentence. A balance must be struck.

Clip Art
Graphics Ready-to-Use

These are pictures or graphics specially drawn for inclusion in published documents. Many pieces come free with EPDos but others must be bought separately. The advantages are two-fold. Clip-art allows non-artists to include hand-drawn illustrations in their publications and they are free of copyright once purchased. A cheap but effective way of improving documents.

Crop Marks
The Boundaries of a Page Size

If you print pages on over-sized paper, crop marks can be printed to show the true size of the desired page. For example, you may want an A5 page size in the end (this book is A5 but have a printer that will only take the much larger A4. When printing, Crop Marks will show you where the final output should be cut or Cropped.

Cropping
Cutting a Page or Graphic Down to Size

Cropping (see above) also refers to the practice or removing unwanted or unnecessary detail out of pictures or graphics. For example, you may want a head-and-shoulders picture of someone but only have a full-height photo. The rest of the body can be Cropped Out.

Cutting

Deletion of an Object from a Page

You may decide that you no longer like or require an object, be it text or graphic, on a page. You can 'Cut' this out by selecting it with the mouse and then choosing the Cut feature to remove it. The item can be retrieved by Pasting as long as nothing else is Cut or Copied.

Curves

Text on an Unstraight Line

Text does not have to follow straight lines. It can be set up to follow the bend in a curve.

Distortions

Text that Grows or Shrinks

By increasing the size of characters at one end of a sentence compared to the other, you can achieve a Distorted effect. This can often stand out on a page when all the other text is undistorted. Mainly used for banners and headlines.

Duplicating

Repeating an Item Once or Many Times

The replication of graphics or pieces of text on a page. This can be used to give a 'wallpaper pattern' effect or to stress something important. Replicated items can be increased in size each time and positioned automatically . This can lead to a 'chorus line' effect.

Editing

Making Sure a Story is Correct

One of the most important tasks in DTP is to ensure accuracy of stories. Even if only used within an organisation, a story could cause considerable distress if inaccurate and lead to legal problems. Part of an editor's job is to decide what can and cannot be said. Some of the tasks of an editor are given to Subs (Sub-Editors) and Proof-Readers. They will check for general accuracy and grammatical use.

Equating

Ensuring Two Objects are the Same Size

Sometimes you may want two or more objects to be exactly the same size. Doing this by eye and hand is extremely inaccurate and subjective. A tool exists in EPDos to allow you to do this automatically and precisely. This is extremely useful if you have decided that all pictures will be the a standard size in your design.

Fills

Patterns and Textures for Objects

To make the shapes you draw more visually interesting or distinctive, you can apply a pattern or 'texture' that will cover the enclosed surface. In EPDos you will find over seventy patterns divided into lines, greys and 'macintosh'. These can be applied to boxes, rounded boxes and ellipses plus some of the TextEffect graphics.

Flippping

The Mirror-Image of Objects

A graphic or picture can be mirrored on a page. This gives the effect of reversing left and right or up and down. The image can be returned to its normal or original way round at any time. If you want original and mirrored images together you must copy first.

Fonts

Typeface, Attribute and Size Combined

This is a set of characters (alphabetic, numeric, grammatical and special of the same basic design or Typeface) combined with an attribute such as Italics or Bold and of the same size. The text you are now reading is 10 point Times New Roman Normal. This is 10 point Times New Roman Italic. See also Typeface, Italics, Bold, Attribute, Serif, Sans Serif, Point.

Footers

A Line of Text to End Each Page

In a document, a Footer rounds of each page with information useful to the reader. Often it will contain the page number, the document title, the chapter or section title and possibly the date of publication. See Header.

Frames

An Area Designated for Text.

This is an area or box on the page which has been drawn with the mouse and is effectively set aside for text entry. When you start typing it will be in the top left-hand corner and the text will continue on the next line whenever you hit the right-hand margin. Within a frame you can apply different fonts and styles. See Linking, Unlinking and Aligning.

Grid

An Invisible Matrix on a Page

To help you line items up and keep to a format more easily, you can show a Grid on screen. This is not printed out and consists of tiny stars ('+') at regular intervals that you can define. See Snap To Grid.

Header

A Line of Text to End Each Page

In a document, a Header starts off each page with information useful to the reader. Often it will contain the page number, the document title, the chapter or section title and possibly the date of publication. See Footer.

Headlines

Eye-Catching Attention-Grabbers

A phrase deliberately designed to catch the reader's attention and tell them what the article or chapter is about (except in tabloid journalism where the rule is to sensationalise even the most mundane news).

Hyphenation

Splitting a Word Between Two Lines

When a word will not properly fit on one line but would leave big gaps if put completely on the next, the word can be split with a dash to balance both text lines.

Italics

The Slanting of a Typeface for Effect

A typeface that has a slope to the right as if the letters and characters are falling over. It is useful in distinguishing a word or phrase from the surrounding text. Italics give a more dramatic feel to a piece of text.

Image-Setter

An Ultra-High Quality Printer

Way beyond the realms of the average DTP user. Both the print resolution and the precision of placing are extremely high. Costing many thousands of pounds, they are used in the printing, publishing and advertising trades. Give almost photographic quality reproduction.

Justification

How a Column of Text is Lined Up

A column of text can be lined up to the left, right or centre as demonstrated below. Be warned, however, that different DTP and word-processing packages may use different terminology. Some call this 'alignment'. EPDos also allows vertical justification of Text Frames to top, bottom and middle.

Left-justified text is flush to the left-hand side of the Text Frame whilst the right-hand side is ragged.

Right-justification is the opposite.

Justified text is flush down both sides although incomplete lines will be left justified. The space between words and letters is adjusted to ensure evenness.

Force Justified text will make even incomplete lines   flush   on   both   sides.

Centred or Middle Justification is where the line is balanced on either side of the central line of the column. It is ragged both left and right.

29

Kerning

Adjusting Space Between Character Pairs

The shape of certain characters means that they have special rules for governing the amount of space between them when combined. A good example is the pair of letters 'W' and 'A'. The normal spacing rules leave an excessive gap so this is reduced, i.e., 'WA' not 'W A'.

Landscape

A Page Wider than It is Tall

A 'horizontal' page that is wider than it is tall. So-called because this is the normal orientation for landscape paintings. See Portrait.

Leading

The Space Between Lines of Text

Pronounced 'ledding' not 'leeding'. A phrase dating back to the time when lines of lead metal were inserted between lines of text to separate them before pressing. This greatly affects how readable a paragraph is and the space required for a piece of text.

It is measured in between Baselines and in EPDos as a percentage of the font size. For example, a 20-point font with 120% Leading would leave a gap of 4 points.

Letter-Spacing

Extra Spacing Between Characters

Putting extra spaces between characters in order to add effect or emphasis.

Lines

Straight Lines Made Easy

A drawing tool to ensure that lines drawn are straight.

Linking

Flow Text Between Frames Automatically

Two or more Text Frames can be 'joined'. They are not joined in the sense that they touch each other on the page. Instead, when you have filled one frame with text, you will automatically jump to the start of the next frame in the chain. Similarly, if you modify one frame, it will often affect text in the following ones.

Logo

A Symbol to Represent an Organisation

Short for Logotype, it means a design or symbol that is used to represent an organisation, often containing its initials. Aims to make recognition easier.

Lower-Case

letters not capitalised

the term originates from the days when small letters were kept in the lower of two boxes or cases. see UPPERCASE.

30

Margins — Edge or Border on a Page

Most layouts and designs call for an area of empty space around the main body of text and/or graphics. Only for design purposes would text go right up to the edge of a page or Bleed off it but graphics often go to the edge and beyond. This technique is most widely used in fashion and consumer magazines, particularly on the cover. Unfortunately, many printers have a built-in margin.

Marks — System for Indicating Changes to Proofs

As Proof-Reader and publisher are rarely the same person in publishing, a standard system of correction marks has developed over the years. This industry short-hand allows both parties to understand the corrections to be made to the next proofs. These are contained in the Writer's Handbook' published by Macmillan/PEN.

Object — A Piece of Text or Graphical Image

EPDos works by creating and manipulating Objects whether they are made of text or photos or hand-drawn pictures. These objects can be moved around on the page and it is the interaction of these that gives the design element to a layout. They effectively break a document down into manageable, related chunks of information.

Object Specification — Control and Format of an Object

If an object or item on a page has to conform to an exact format, you can use this facility for precise control. You have control over positioning and size plus whether it can be printed, locked into position etc.

Overlapping — Part of an Item Goes over Another Item

Items do not need to be kept completely separate in DTP. They can touch and run over each over. The part underneath can be either completely obscured or mixed in with the one on top. See Stacking, Wrapping.

Paragraph Spacing — Distinguishes Paragraphs from Lines

An extra amount of space between the last line of one paragraph and the start of the next, used to distinguish the end of the paragraph.

Without this extra space, it would be harder to spot natural breaks in the text. This is not the same as putting a blank line between paragraphs.

Pasting	### Putting an Item or Object in Place

Originally a publishing term from when glue was used to fasten items of text or graphic in position on a page. Now used in computing parlance to mean transferring an item from the computer's Clipboard (having previously been Cut or Copied) and onto the document

Picas

A Measure of Typeface Size

There are six Picas to one inch and twelve points to a Pica. There for a 12-point font is also a 1-Pica font.

Point

A Very Small Measure of Typeface Size

Basic Typeface measure. One seventy-second of an inch. Twelve Points make a Pica.

Polygons

Many-Sided Shapes

EPDos allows you to create regular Polygons which you can fill with text. This text is automatically centred and Polygons can have a number of sides from three upwards.

Portrait

A Page that is Taller than it is Wide

This is the normal page format where the height is greater than the width. So-called because this is the normal format for photographers taking head-and-shoulders or Portraits. See Landscape

PostScript

Laser Language for Describing a Page

This is a method of producing a page on a lasers printer. Each object or item is given a description and these are put together in the printer's memory to create a complete page. PostScript is very powerful and flexible and seen as the mark of a professional laser printer.

PostScript's other advantage is that it has become a standard for commercial printing bureaus. They can take a document stored on disk and print it out on ultra-high quality Image-setters and other equipment.

Presets

Standard Layouts for Users

Most DTP systems come with a series of ready-made page layouts that you can use as-is or modify. They make an excellent starting point for novice users.

EPDos has a number of Presets and you can also define your own Custom Pages if you wish.

Proof-Reading   Checking a Proof for Accuracy

Ensuring that text is correct grammatically, makes sense and is laid out properly. Similarly, that graphics are correctly positioned, Cropped accurately etc.

Proofs   Trial Print Runs

Having designed your document on the screen, you will want to see it 'in the flesh' by printing it out. It is unlikely to be perfect first time so you will need to correct it by making marks in read on the page. These are known as Proof-Marks and help you to go back and alter the layout and text on the screen.

Proportional   Measuring Space Between Lines

See Baseline, Leading.

Punctuation Marks   Pauses, Questions , Emphatic Stresses

Several of these characters are included in a typeface to allow the reader or speaker to draw breath or pause. Others add stress or an inquisitive tone. They also break text up into blocks that can be managed more easily. Good punctuation enhances understanding.

Punctuation Marks include the;

Full Stop	.
Comma	,
Colon	:
Semi-Colon	;
Exclamation	!
Question	?
Apostrophe	'
Quotation	"
Parenthesis	( )

Reversed Colours   Black Becomes White & Vice-Versa

For dramatic effect, a picture can often look more effective if it is reversed. Most printing is really small areas of black on a white background so anything that opposes this stands out.

However, most printers, even lasers, are poor at printing large expanses of black so this should be used sparingly.

Reversed-Out   White Text on a Black Background

Often used for headers and headlines, white characters are 'printed' while the background is filled in as black. See Reversed Colours.

33

Rotate

Turning an Item Around an Axis

You can alter the orientation of an object on a page in most DTP programs. In EPDos, you can rotate graphical objects by 90 degrees to the right (clockwise), left (anti-clockwise) and by 180 degrees so that it is upside-down. The TextEffect program allows you to rotate headlines and objects by any factor you choose. This gives far better control.

Sans Serif

A Typeface Without Fancy Bits

The typeface on the line above is Sans Serif. Simple and plain typeface.

Scaling

Keeping Objects in Proportion

If you want you want to enlarge or reduce an object, you often want to retain the proportion of the sides to the top. You may also want to, for example, double the overall side lengths exactly. This can be achieved automatically by applying a Scaling Factor e.g. 200%

It is important to not that this factor applies to lengths and not areas. A factor of 200% would double lengths but quadruple areas. To double the area you would need to enter the square root of 200.

Send To Back

Putting An Object on the Bottom of a Pile

If you have a complex image made up of several objects on top of each other then you can put one object underneath all the others.

Serif

Extensions to Letter-Stokes

A Serif typeface has thin lines added to the unconnected ends of letter-strokes as with the text you are now reading. These are embellishments that in some ways are unnecessary but add to the decorativeness of a typeface. They can also be used to distinguish between headlines and the main text of a story or article.

Separations

Many Colours Made from the Few

The whole spectrum is, in essence, made up of only three colours. When mixed in different strengths, these can create all others. The exception is black which is the absence of light.

There are different conventions for defining colours. T.V. screens and monitors use RGB (Red-Green-Blue) components whilst photographers prefer CMY (Cyan-Magenta-Yellow).

Printing has its own conventions but Image-setters use the strengths of each colour component to determine final colour. These are called the Separations i.e., the components have been separated.

Shuffle

Moving Objects Up and Down the Pile

Where several objects are placed on top of each other on a page, the order can have an effect on the composite image. Shuffle Up will move a selected object one layer nearer the top of the pile. Shuffle Down will move it one layer lower down.

Snap To Grid

An Aid to Accurate Placing of Objects

The Grid that can be shown on the screen in EPDos can be used for automatic fine positioning of objects. With this facility switched on, any object will be moved to the nearest marker on the grid.

Solid

An Object Not Mixed With Others

An object can be made solid so that any objects below it in a pile do not show through.

Speech Marks

Another Word for Quotation Marks

The punctuation mark " used to denote the text was spoken or is part of a quotation.

Stacking

Objects in Layers

Objects can be placed one on top of another in a Stack or pile on a page. Not every detail from every object is likely to be printed. See Solid, Transparent, Shuffle, Send to Back, Bring to Front.

Stories

Continuous Text of Article, Chapter etc.

A term used to describe all the text linked together. In a newsletter, this would consist of complete articles regardless of however many columns or frames were used. In a book, a whole chapter of linked text would be considered as a Story for editing purposes.

Styles

The Formatting of Paragraphs

In most documents, it is normal to have standard typefaces, fonts and ways of laying out paragraphs. Often there can be several different combinations which serve to distinguish different types of story or their importance. These combinations can be remembered by EPDos and applied to individual paragraphs or whole stories. Each combination or Style can also be given its own name.

Subhead
Reeling the Reader In
If the headline serves to 'hook' the reader, then the sub-heading is designed to 'reel' them in. In size and style, it is usually twice the size of the main text or more but far smaller than the headline. It should give an outline of the contents of the article.

Tabulation
Off-Setting Text
Tabulation is used to offset one piece of text from others. This makes it stand out better and is often used to indicate a list of items or points to be made. Tab Marks have to be preset and each press of the Tab key moves the text one Tab along. Tabs can be formatted so that text appears to the left, right or is centred about the mark. Decimal tabs denote where the decimal points in a list of numbers will be lined up. This is very useful in DTP.

Templates
Pre-Defined Page /Document Layouts
See Presets.

Tilde
The Wavy Accent for 'yghh' Sounds
In Portuguese and Spanish, this accent appears above certain letters such as the 'N' to turn the pronunciation from 'nghh' to 'nyghh'.

Titles
The Name of a Document
A word frequently used in the publishing industry to mean an individual publication. 'Women's Own' is a Title as is 'Mechanics Weekly'. Publishing companies buy and sell Titles. Often the Title name is put at the top or bottom of each page. See Header, Footer.

Top of Caps
Measuring Space Between Lines
See Baseline, Leading.

Tracking
Spacing Between Letters in Text
Tracking controls the overall spacing between letters in a piece of text. Tight Tracking brings all the letters closer together and compacts the text. Loose Tracking spaces letters out and takes up more room.

Transparent
Allowing Objects Underneath to Show
If an object is made Transparent, then any objects underneath will show through and the details of both will be printed together. It is as if the object were printed on see-through plastic such as OHP sheets. See Solid.

Typeface　　　## The Form of the Characters

The typeface is the most distinctive feature of a font and gives the character 'character'. Faces can be fancy or plain, brash or subtle, broad or fine. Designing a face is an art and designers can spend long periods of time just making sure every stroke and line is perfectly consistent.

Umlaut　　　## German Accent on Letters

This 'double-dot' accent has the effect of extending the marked vowel by an 'e'.

Units　　　## Measurements within a Document

Traditional printing measurements have been in Picas and Points but in DTP systems you can usually use inches and centimetres.

Unlinking　　　## Breaking the Chain of Two Text Frames

Frames that have connected text can be separated so that the end of one no longer runs into the next.

UPPER-CASE　　　## CAPITAL LETTERS

The term originates from the days when small letters were kept in the upper of two boxes or cases. see Lower-Case.

Wrapping Text　Text Following the Contours of a Picture

Many pictures are square in shape and fitting text to this is simple as the margin is straight. However, other pictures have empty spaces and text can be fitted into this area even if it is an odd shape. This is called Wrapping.

B. **The Express Publisher Screen**

```
File Edit Text Page Objects Options Help          UNTITLED.EPD
```

```
Press ALT to choose commands                              Page  1
```

B1. Icons

Pictures to Help Understanding

An Icon is a small picture that helps you choose the feature you want. The picture is designed to make its purpose obvious. To choose a particular feature, you either single or double-click on it.

In EPDos, the Toolbox is a line of icons each doing different jobs. These are listed and explained below.

The Pointer Tool

The Moveable Arrow for Selecting Items

To perform certain actions on an items, you must usually select the item first. Obviously, EPDos needs to know which item you want changing.

If, for example, you have been entering text, the cursor will have changes to one suitable for text entry but not for selecting items. When you want to select an item, you must move the mouse pointer to the Pointer Tool Icon and click. The cursor will change to a diagonal pointer.

By holding the CNTRL key whilst you select items, you will he able to choose more than one item at a time.

The Text Tool

The Cursor for Text Entry

The cursor for normal text entry is known as the 'I-Beam' and is the shape of a fancy letter I with a horizontal bar across the lower half. This is used to select the position of text to be typed in rather than where the text is currently being typed in. This can seem confusing. The straight I shaped cursor is where actual typing takes place and the I-Beam allows you to move around the text frame to where you want to type next.

The I-Beam can also be used to mark areas of text for deletion, copying, pasting etc. Editing is much easier as you can move from one part of the frame to another or to a completely different frame on the page.

Text Frame Tool — *The Position and Sizing of Blocks of Text*

In EPDos, text can only be entered into previously-defined' Frames'. Clicking on the Text Frame Tool turns the cursor into a 'pencil' which you use to draw the shape and position of the frame you want to type text in.

The rectangular shape marked out forms the boundaries or any text entered although these can be modified later using the Pointer Tool. The thick black lines around a text frame do not print out. They are merely a visual guide while you are laying out on-screen.

Frames can be good and bad. they allow you to design the layout of a page very accurately and you can then fit your text to them. However, if you do not know how long your text is and do not want it editing to fit a particular space, you must keep re-sizing or linking to other frames.

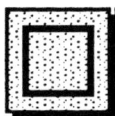

Box Tool — *Creating Rectangles and Boxes*

Boxes are commonly used in publications to mark off certain areas of a page and can act as the surrounds for pictures and graphics. They are also useful for showing that certain items are linked together.

For example, a page of text about a certain topic may have a box containing definitions of the terms used. Sometimes these are shaded in to strengthen the effect. To ensure a perfect square you need only press the CNTRL key as you alter the size.

Rounded Box Tool — *Giving Rectangles a Softer Edge*

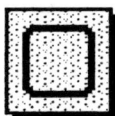

Boxes with squared corners can often look too harsh and repetitive. By rounding the corners off even just a little, the effect can be more informal and easier on the eye. The degree of rounding can be varied to an extent but it is best to stick to one format on a page and preferably in a document as a whole. To ensure the squareness, hold down the CNTRL key while changing the size.

39

Ellipse Tool

Drawing Circles and Ellipses

One of the most useful shapes in terms of design is the ellipse or circle. These can be used to draw diagrams and are often used in logos to give the effect of a 'seal' or guarantee. For a perfect circle, you need only keep the CNTRL key depressed when changing the size.

Line Tool

Drawing Straight Lines at Various Angles

Most people find freehand drawing very difficult. Normally you would use a ruler and pen but on a computer you only have a mouse. Using the Line Tool ensures straight lines to whatever length and angle you require every time.

Set Line Tool

Changing the Thickness of a Line

This tool allows you to change the thickness of a line drawn using one of the other drawing tools. Different thicknesses are available from the very fin to the very thick. Beyond this, using the Box Tool filled in is more effective. Fine lines show that an object is still part of the main text or design on a page but distinguish it subtly. Thick lines show that something is separate completely.

Set Fill Tool

Adding Texture to a Shape

Having drawn a shape using the tools above, you can use various shadings or 'fills' to add texture or distinguish between different elements such as the foreground and background. Shadow effects can be created by creating a box filled in with a dark shading and then drawing a similar box over the top using a lighter shade.

Link Tool

Connecting Blocks of Text Together

On a page or in a document as a whole, you will probably have to split text up into various blocks even though they are connected by the storyline. To ensure continuity, you must link all the text frames together. This way, if you edit one frame then all the others change automatically.

For example, if you wish to remove a paragraph that is part of a story spread over several pages. You would not want to move all the other text about to compensate for this change. By linking the frames, all text will move up automatically. This is extremely fast compared to doing it manually.

You must be careful, however, that the formatting still looks good. It is essential to check the changes made.

Unlink Tool

Separating Text Frames

Whereas the Link Tool creates a 'flow' of text between frames, the Unlink Tool interrupts it. Having created a story, you may wish to treat some parts of it as separate items. To do this you unlink them. Thus, any changes made to the main story will have no effect whatsoever on the part that has be 'unlinked'.

Align Tool

Positioning Text Frames

Often it is desirable to have frames of text lined up next to each other. Doing this by eye is often difficult and what appears on the screen comes out slightly different on paper. To save this hassle and aggravation, you can use this tool to automatically line two frames up with each other. Then you should be able to print them exactly.

Equate Tool

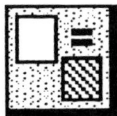

Text Frames of the Same Size

Text frames often look as if they are related to each other if they have the same dimensions. By the same token, you may wish to give the same weight to two sides of an argument. This can be done effectively by making the size of the frames equal. This is difficult by eye so this tool does it for you.

Text Wrap Tool

For Combining Text and Graphics Better

This is one of the most important tools for design. It allows you to combine text and graphics in a variety of ways. For example, you may want a small picture of a person being profiled to appear between two columns of text about his background. Rather than break the text in both columns and jump over the picture, you can have the text fit itself to the pictures size and shape. This is known as 'Text Wrapping'.

Modern publications are full of this kind of effect. Alternatively, you can specify that text jumps any picture or that the two are mixed together although this can look very messy if not done carefully.

TextEffect

Launching the Graphics Package

This is not strictly a tool. TextEffects is the 'sister' package that comes with EPDos. It allows you to create much more advances pictures than EPDos and these can then be brought back into the main document. By clicking on this icon you are launching TextEffect and suspending EPDos until you return.

41

B2. Menus

More Options to Choose From

The second line down of the screen is known as the 'Menu Line'. This contains all the options available to you which were not suitable to be made into tool icons. Each Menu has many choices contain in it. These are revealed by clicking on them. A detailed knowledge of them is not necessary at this stage so only a brief description is given below. Each feature is described in detail later on.

The File Menu

| File | Edit | Text | Pag |
| New... |
| Open... |
| Open Template... |
| Import Text... |
| Import Picture... |
| Close |
| Save |
| Save As... |
| Save As Picture... |
| Choose Printer... |
| Print... |
| Exit |

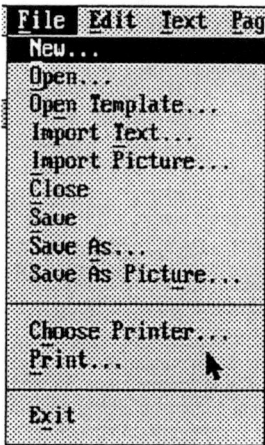

Storing, Retrieving and Printing

The options in the File Menu allow you to start a new document as well as retrieve existing ones from your computers hard or floppy disks.

You can also bring in pictures and text created in other programs such as graphics packages and word-processors. This means that the same items can be used in different documents without needing to be re-created. Many use this to create styles across different publications and add in logos and photos scanned in electronically.

The File Menu also controls how you print out your documents and ensures that the printer understands the information it is receiving.

When you have finished with the document, you can exit from EPDos altogether.

The Edit Menu

| Edit | Text | Page | Obje |
| Undo Move |
| Cut |
| Copy |
| Paste |
| Duplicate |
| Duplicate Many... |
| Select Entire Story |
| Search/Replace |
| Clear Clipboard |
| Show Clipboard |

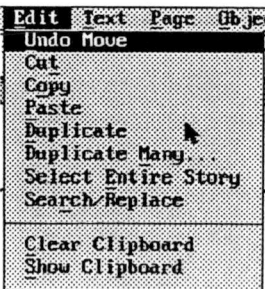

Manipulating Objects

When you have created an item within a document, often you will need to change it in some way or even get rid of it totally. On the other hand, you may want to move it or make copies. The latter can be either single copies or multiple copies where the image is repeated and may be re-sized or 'tiled' across a page.

The Edit Menu also allows you to select an entire story so that you can do the same thing to all the frames linked together. For example, you may want to change the font. You can also find or change phrases within a story.

Objects can also be saved temporarily to a section of the computer's main memory known as the 'Clipboard'.

If you make a mistake, the Edit Menu usually allows you to 'Undo' it: this is a life-saver in many circumstances.

The Text Menu

```
Text  Page  Objects  Op
Choose Font...
Choose Style...
Create Style...
Delete Style...

Justify Text...  ▶
Set Tabs...
Hyphenation...
Text Frame Margins

Kerning...
Character Spacing..
Line Spacing...
Paragraph Spacing...
```

Customising Characters

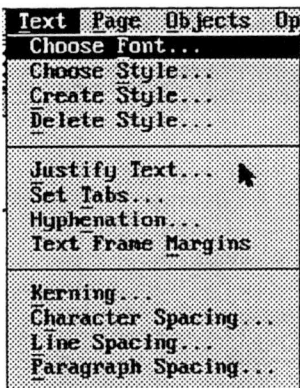

Making sure that the 'look and feel' of text is just right is one of the most important and difficult parts of DTP. There are so many components that go to making a story look right that whole books have been written on the subject. Professional page layout designers spend long periods of time trying out different combinations of typeface, size and spacing to suit the publication.

EPDos contains all the facilities you are likely to need to achieve the right result but it is up to you to ensure the final result is pleasing to the eye of the reader.

Options allow you to change font, paragraph layout and spacing to suit your designs.

The Page Menu

```
Page  Objects  Options  He
Zoom In
·Actual Size
Zoom Out
Show Page  ▶

New Page...
Delete Page...
Previous Page    F3
Next Page        F4
Go to Page...    F5

Headers and Footers...
Insert Header or Footer
```

Moving Around Documents

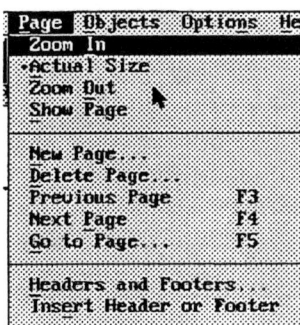

Most users will have screens that are much smaller than the document to be printed. This means a compromise has to be struck. You can choose between seeing a small section of a page but full-size or the whole page with everything shrunken. The former is useful for fine editing and the latter for seeing the overall effect.

You also need to move around the pages contained within a document as well as to be able to add new pages and delete old ones.

The Page Menu also allows you to add standard items such as Headers and Footers at the top and bottom of every page, essential for continuous page numbering.

The Objects Menu

```
Objects  Options  Help
Bring to Front    CTRL+F
Send to Back      CTRL+E
Shuffle Up
Shuffle Down  ▶

Reverse Colors
Edit Bit Image
Crop Image
Split Text Frame...

Rotate Object...
Flip Object...
Scale Object...    F9
Object Specs...
```

Manipulating Images

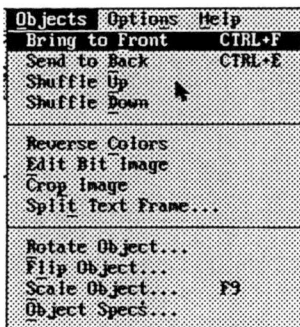

Images are often built up of several objects on top of one another. For example, to create a simple sunset, you draw a circle and then place a rectangle over the bottom half of it. The order of these 'layers' can be very important in determining the final image. Therefore you need control over which layer goes where and the 'shuffling' and other options allow this.

Other choices allow you greater control over the Image by altering details down to the level of the individual dots that make up a picture.

The Objects Menu also much greater manipulation so that you can create mirror images or rotate them. You can also specify size precisely.

The Options Menu Customising the Screen Area

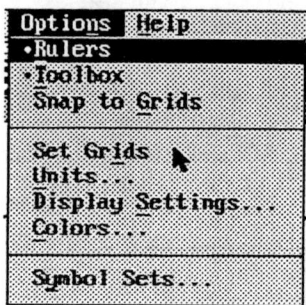

Options Help
• Rulers
• Toolbox
Snap to Grids

Set Grids
Units...
Display Settings...
Colors...

Symbol Sets...

The ability to change the way the standard EPDos screen looks is extremely useful. For example, if you monitor is black and white then certain 'colour' combinations can make seeing the information very difficult.

You may also not want some of the facilities normally available such as the rulers. Removing these allows a larger working area; useful if your screen is small. You can also choose the units of measurements you want to work. If you have previous publishing experience then you can use the standard industry measuring conventions. Otherwise you can use good old metric.

The Help Menu Essential Guidance

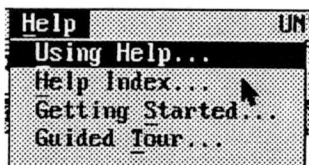

Help   UN
Using Help...
Help Index...
Getting Started...
Guided Tour...

Even experienced users can forget how to do something and beginners will probably use the Help Menu almost as often as any other. One advantage of this 'on-line' facility is that it is always there. It not only act as a backup to the manual but often explains things in a different manner. If you don't understand one, the chances are you'll understand the other.

B3. Function Key Shortcuts

Keyboard Shortcuts are designed to speed things up by cutting out the need to search for the right menu option. The irony is that menus and mice were devised to cut out the need to remember the right combination of keys for a particular feature. That's life as they say!

In EPDos Illustrated, a conscious avoidance of these has been made for several reasons. Firstly, that the Quick Reference Card (or crib-sheet) contains both menus and shortcuts but on opposite sides of the sheet thereby minimising the advantages of combining both methods. Secondly, there is no template to fit over the keys themselves. Thirdly, it is less confusing to remember just one way of working. Finally, it has been much easier to design exercises using just one method.

B4. Text and Dialog Keys

The normal keyboard controls are available such as tab, backspace, delete, cursor control, home/end/page up and page down. Using the CNTRL keys moves you about the whole story. When using a dialog box, tab moves you to a different question whilst left and right change the choice. enter (or carriage return) accepts the option.

C. The TextEffect Screen

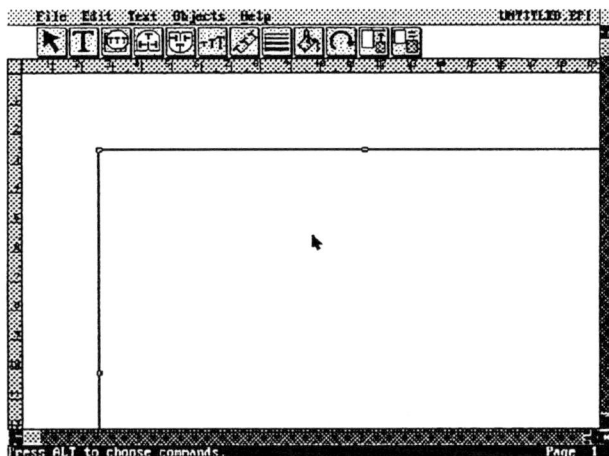

C1. Icons

Artistic Freedom

Both EPDos and TextEffect have some icons and Tool-box features in common. These are the Pointer, Text, Set Line, Set Fill, Align and Equate.

Note that TextEffect is not set up to handle paragraphs or text frames. Instead, it lets you add special effects to phrases, sentences and individual words. It is much more artistic then EPDos. The Text tool, for instance, allows you to put shadow and other effects on letters.

The Polygon Tool

Many-Sided Shapes Containing Text

Polygons can have any number of sides from three (a triangle) to thirty. Within these, you can use this feature to put a line of text which is automatically centred.

However large or small the polygon, the text always remains centred.

Curve Up/Down

Bending Text.

Many logos and designs call for the name or some detail to be curved rather than sitting on a flat line. The degree of the curvature can be changed both up an down.

With Curve Down, the text will run clockwise but with Curve Up the text runs anti-clockwise. In other words, the text always runs from the left to right.

45

The Distortion Tool

Growing and Shrinking Text

This effect allows each characters in a phrase to be larger or smaller than its immediate neighbour. This can give an effect of the text shrinking into the distance or expanding to the forefront. It is highly effective in stressing the word which is writ largest and making the phrase stand out from the rest if used in moderation.

The Line Tool

Slanting Text

With this tool, you can make text appear to run either uphill or down hill. This breaks up the normal horizontal pattern of texts and can be used to give a 'cut-out and stuck-on' appearance if you want it.

The Rotate Tool

Spinning Objects Around

Just as the Line Tool can put text at an angle, the Rotate Tool allows you to spin any object about its axis through the full wheel of 360 degrees. This is a feature not always found in even top-end DTP packages.

C2. Menus

More Options to Choose From

As with EPDos proper, the second line down from the top of the screen contains a menu line. This contains a number of options that are not included as icons. However, the TextEffect menus are not as comprehensive due to it being limited to only text and image manipulation rather than page or document handling.

The File Menu

Starting, Adding and Saving Graphics

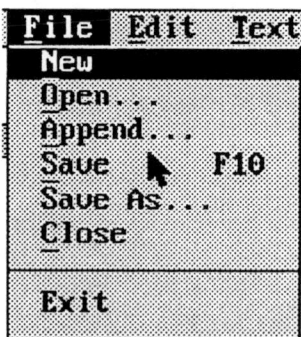

With this menu, you can start a new graphic, load an old one or add another image into the design. When you have finished, you can save the image, close the file and exit back to the main EPDos program.

```
File  Edit  Text
New
Open...
Append...
Save        F10
Save As...
Close

Exit
```

The Help Menu

Getting You Out of Difficulty

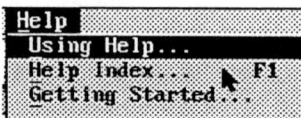

Should you experience problems achieving a particular result, you can always call up the built-in Help Screen on virtually any topic TextEffect deals with.

```
Help
Using Help...
Help Index...    F1
Getting Started...
```

The Edit Menu

```
 Edit  Text
 Undo Move

 Cut
 Copy
 Paste
 Duplicate
```

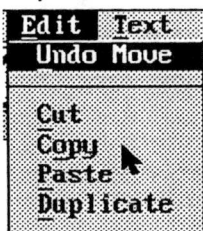

Adding, Subtracting, Repeating Objects

This menu is the electronic equivalent of an eraser, a pair of scissor and a photocopier. If you do something wrong you can erase the action.

You can remove parts of an image that do not fit in properly or just move them elsewhere. You may also repeat an item either once or many times on the worksheet.

The Text Menu

```
 Text  Objects  Help
 Choose Font...

 Justify Text...

 Kerning...
 Character Spacing...
```

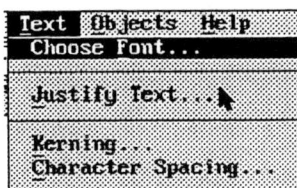

Modifying Characters and Phrases

TextEffect deals with short phrases or pieces of text. These can be modified so that different typefaces, sizes, styles, etc.

This degree of control greatly enhances the final result.

The Objects Menu

```
 Objects  Help
 Bring to Front   CTRL+F
 Send to Back     CTRL+E

 Shuffle Up
 Shuffle Down
 Rotate Object...
 Scale Object...  F9
```

Controlling Overlap

Frequently, you will need to build up an image layer upon layer. When all are in place, you should have the graphic you desire. This requires a large degree of control of which element is where. Using the 'Send' and 'Shuffle' commands you can do this more easily and effectively.

This menu also gives you precise control over how much an object is rotated and its size.

C3. Keyboard Shortcuts

Some of the short-cut keys in EPDos are also available in TextEffect. However, for the same reasons mentioned earlier, these are not discussed in detail here. They can all be found on the Quick Reference Card supplied with the package.

Chapter 3.   Introducing Desk Top Publishing

A.   The History of D.T.P.
A1.   Pre-Electronic Publishing   49
A2.   The Arrival of Computers   49
A3.   Computer Power Increases   51
A4.   The 'Friendlier Face' of Computers   51
A5.   The First Practical D. T. P. Systems   51
A6.   Current D. T. P. Systems   51

B.   What Is Desk Top Publishing ?
B1.   The Hardware and Software Needed   52
B2.   The Skills Needed to Become a D. T. Per   52
B3.   The Elements of D. T. P.   53

C.   What Use is Desk Top Publishing ?
C1.   In Business and At Work   55
C2.   In the Home And for Personal Use   55
C3.   Schools, Societies and Organisations   55

D.   The Concepts and Ideas Used in D.T.P.
D1.   Fonts, Typefaces, Sizes and Type Styles   56
D2.   Tracking, Kerning and Leading   56
D3.   Paragraph Styles, Indents and Tabs   57
D4.   Hyphenation and Alignment   57
D5.   Columns, Guides, Rulers and Grids   57
D6.   Lines, Shapes, Fills and Wraps   58
D7.   Image Control, Back, Front   58
            and Transparent

A. The History of D. T. P.

A1. Pre-Electronic Publishing

Printed documents have been around for hundreds of years. The earliest examples are now worth a fortune. The effort and skill that went in to producing a complete publication was immense. Publishing was truly a handcraft. Pages were made up character-by-character.

Book publishing at its best allowed the great works to be seen by a much wider audience and some of the early engravings (carved by hand) remain potent images today. Indeed, if it had not been for the early publishing industry, many of the most influential works in the fields of the arts, science and politics would never have seen the light of day.

Gradually presses became more automated and this allowed the first regular newspapers to appear. Eventually daily papers became possible. The skills largely remained and the tight deadlines meant working under tremendous pressure. Constant lowering costs meant that books and papers were no longer the preserve of the fortunate few. Education widened its reach.

A2. The Arrival of Computers

However, despite gradual changes in the technology, the pace of development reached a plateau several decades ago. It was the arrival of the micro-computer that really shook things up. At the start, they could merely handle simple text; they were little more than electronic typewriters whose finished product left much to be desired.

Then, in the mid-Eighties, the Apple Macintosh arrived on the scene and brought a whole new way of working with it. The computer was no longer simply seen as a manipulator of numbers and text (a glorified calculator). Instead, it started to work in pictures and images. Not only were the features of the computer expressed in the graphic icons, but the computer could be used to draw pictures and incorporate photographs etc.

The all-singing, all-dancing computer had arrived. You could now see on the screen the results you wanted to achieve. This was a huge advance.

A3. Computer Power Increases

The first DTP systems were of limited use and sophistication. They certainly had more facilities than the word-processors but it was usually obvious when DTP had been used rather than the traditional printing methods.

A major advance was the introduction of the Laser Printer. This allowed users to print out precisely what was on the screen and the leap in quality compare to other forms of printer was tremendous. Lasers print out ten times more accurately than the popular dot-matrices.

A4. The 'Friendlier Face' of Computers

Despite the improved methods of working with computers, the first packages were aimed at publishing companies and often tailored to their specific needs. They were expensive and involved a long learning process.

However, they soon became popular and costs fell rapidly in line with the fall in computer prices. The Macintosh owes it success to the DTP revolution. For many years it was the only real justification for buying one but the increased sales reduced costs.

Packages were soon produced that were much more powerful but also allowed a far more natural way of handling images and creating documents. This boosted DTP enormously.

A5. The First Practical D. T. P. Systems

Soon the costs were bring DTP into the price range of mere mortals. They also transferred from the Macintosh to the PC which further brought costs down as the market was so much larger.

One hindrance to DTP was that, on the PC, each manufacturer created their own style. This was particularly so of programs running in Dos. However, the programs did start to resemble each other more and more as each producer tried to outdo rivals.

Armed with a second or third generation PC plus a dot-matrix printer, it was possible to achieve passable results. Many firms used them despite the lack of quality. They allowed the fast production of advertising and informational materials which included a degree of design that only a proper printer could have done before.

A6. Current D. T. P. Systems

Most established DTP packages are now on at least their second generation and possibly more. The highly-priced ones even more. They most basic can produce excellent results and low-cost bubble-jet printers give a print-out almost as good as that of a laser printer.

The best systems can be used by individuals, small companies, associations and huge corporations. Many big firms use top-end packages for external promotion and the budget ones for day-to-day material. However, it is often hard to distinguish which was used.

Even a budget package running under Dos, such as EPDos, can give great results if used properly.

B.   What Is Desk Top Publishing ?

B1.   The Hardware and Software Needed

EPDos will run on virtually any PC, no matter how old. Unfortunately, it will run very slowly and look very bad on screen if used on the very oldest. You will also need a hard-disk for storing files which quickly grow in size.

You also need a printer. A dot-matrix is passable but a daisy-wheel useless. A laser is desirable but a bubble-jet is almost as good at a fraction of the price. A good quality screen can save many trips to the opticians.

Subsequent chapters will help you decide what you really need and can afford.

B2.   The Skills Needed to Become a D. T. Publisher

The skills needed for successful and effective DTP are much more difficult to define. However, you do not need to be a fully-qualified, time-served typesetter or graphic designer to achieve this. Remember, the simplest is often the best. Follow a few basic rules and study your work objectively and you will improve rapidly.

It is often felt that using DTP automatically makes documents better but this is not so. After all, if the written work is confusing to begin with, no amount of flashy printing or good design will make up for this.

If your documents rely heavily on text, such as stones or articles, it would be worth your while doing a few writing exercises. Simple rules apply. Do not use very long sentences. Keep subjects together but don't let paragraphs occupy half a page. Check your spelling, punctuation or grammar (better still, have someone else do it).

Above all, keep in mind your 'audience'. Try and communicate at their 'level' and cater to their demands. You would not present the same material in the same way to a group of children as you would adults.

Other uses of DTP mean that the emphasis is on graphics and pictures rather than on words. Advertising is often a good example. The old adage, 'a picture is word a thousand words', can be true in many cases.

The latter part of this book helps improve your skills.

B3.   *The Elements of D. T. P.*

The main elements of DTP are text and graphics but even these can be sub-divided further.

Text can be in either Artistic or Narrative form. Narrative forms a story with a thread running through it. This is organised usually into headings, sub-headings and paragraphs. You can modify type styles, sizes, position etc. and the shape of paragraphs to a lesser extent. However, most text will remain in 'Block' form.

Artistic text, on the other hand, has a more free-style feel to it. Generally, it will consist of only short sentences or phrases. Such text will have been modified for size etc. but may also have other things done to it such as being made to follow the curve of a shape or be at an angle, skewed, rotated, flipped and generally distorted.

Graphics come in three main flavours. These are Drawn, Informative and Scanned. The most commonly used, Drawn ones, are those created within the DTP package (or a proper graphics package) and then incorporated on to the page. Packages usually contain a few basic drawing tools such as rectangles, ellipses, lines and freehand. Along with shading and 'fills', effective results can be achieved with even the most basic of functions.

Some of these tools an also be used to set the layout of the page. Boxes with side-information can be distinguished from the main text by using a box and shading.

Informative graphics, such as charts and tables, are often created using other computer software such as spreadsheets, databases and presentation packages. These are a pictorial means of conveying important information and are often used to highlight relationships between data. Be warned, however, it is very easy to go overboard. Such graphics should be used sparingly and only when the graphics is more 'expressive' than text.

Scanned graphics have usually been created entirely separate of the computer and read in using a device similar to that used to scan an image on a photocopier. Photographs, hand-drawn illustrations, three-dimensional objects placed on or under a scanner can be incorporated into finished documents. The availability of low -cost hand-scanners has made such graphics much more popular over the last few years.

C.   **What Use is Desk Top Publishing ?**

C1. *In Business and at Work*

Advertising	Art and Words to sell or market goods and services
Propaganda	Reminders e.g., This is a 'No-Smoking Zone'
Education	Written explanations
Training	Part of practical course-work
Stationery	Standard letters, logos, letter-heads, calling cards
Paper Systems	Forms, time-sheets, bureaucracy
Documentation	Accompanying goods and services
Report-writing	Communicating technical information
Informing Colleagues	Social and business events
Magazines	For in-house consumption.

C2. *In the Home and for Personal Use*

Designing Cards	Birthdays, Christmas, etc.
Personalised Stationery	Writing paper with letterheads or even photos
Pleasure	Just for the sheer challenge and enjoyment
Story-writing	Becoming the next Jackie Collins or Jeffrey Archer
Self-Publishing	In the footsteps of many great authors

C3. *Schools, Societies and Organisations*

Newsletters	Letting members know what is happening
Questionnaires	Finding out members' complaints, wishes etc.
Reminders	Coming events, important dates
Campaigns	Political and charitable

D. The Concepts and Ideas Used in D.T.P.

D1. Fonts, Typefaces, Sizes and Type Styles

This is probably the most confusing areas in DTP. Different books and packages can use the same words to mean different things. We shall use the term Font to mean a specific combination of typeface, size and style.

A typeface is the way the different characters in the alphabet have been given the same design. There are two main types or families of typeface; serif and sans serif. Serifs have fancy bits on the ends of character strokes. Sans serif do not.

Size is measured in Points or seventy-seconds of an inch. The larger the number, the larger the image of each character. For books and magazines, text is normally between eight and fourteen point for the main body of the story but much larger for headlines, chapter titles etc.

The Style of the text is seen when the typeface has been modified to lend emphasis or make certain phrases stand out from the rest. Bold text means all the characters are thickened and Italic means they are slanted.

Thus a font is named after the combination of these elements. *10 point Times New Roman Italic* is one such example. Another is **12 point Bahamas Bold.**

D2. Tracking, Kerning and Leading

Tracking determines how close words and letters are together on a line. The 'Tighter' the tracking, the closer the characters are. 'Looser' equals more spaced out.

However, applying the same tracking to every combination of letters would result in some pairings being so far apart it looked like there were two separate words. 'V' and 'A' can be brought closer together because of their respective shapes.

Leading is the amount of space between a line of text and the ones immediately above and below. Tracking is usually measured relative to the type size used. A standard figure is to use 120% of the type size. Thus a 10-point font would stand on a 12-point line. There are different methods of apportioning leading.

D3. Paragraph Styles, Indents and Tabs

Paragraphs are the main unit of Narrative text. They are a collection of sentences (usually related) that are terminated by a Carriage Return . The next paragraph begins on a fresh line.

The text in a paragraph can have several attributes. It can be indented so that it stands away from the edge of the normal block of text. The first line can start either to the left or the right of the following lines.

Tabs or Tabulation allow you to break up a line of text. This is particularly useful when creating tables (hence the name) as you can set the tab positions so that related pieces of information or below one another.

D4. Hyphenation and Alignment

Long words at the end of a line can be broken up into two parts to avoid long gaps between words or at the line end. However, hyphenation should not bed one just anywhere in the word as this can cause misunderstanding. Most long English words are, in reality, formed of several shorter ones and these make natural break points as do consonants or harsher sounds. For example, 'hyphenation' splits into 'hyphen-ation' or even 'hyph-en-ation'.

Alignment is how the starts and ends line up. If only the left side is aligned, the right will appear ragged and vice-versa. When both are aligned, this is called 'Justified' (or 'Forced Justified' if even short ones are lined up on both sides). Centred text will have symmetrical ragged edges.

D5. Columns, Guides, Rulers and Grids

The text in books usually flows across the whole page in one block whereas a magazine will break up this pattern to form vertical columns. You read down one column and then move across to the right for the next.

Guides are lines on the screen that help you format the layout. Each column of text will have a guide line on either side to help position it accurately. These are not usually printed on the final output.

The rulers on the screen further help you place text and graphics by giving to a precise measure of your position on a page. They can be marked in inches, centimetres, picas or points in most packages.

D6. Lines, Shapes, Fills and Wraps

Lines can be used either to split text up or form part of a graphic image. They can be thin or fat, dotted, hached or double. Lines can be at any angle you choose although for accuracy they can be forced into being either horizontal or vertical.

Shapes generally include rectangles, ellipses and rounded boxes. These, too, can be used to distinguish text blocks or as part of an image. Rectangles and ellipses can be forced into squares and circles if needed or the corners simply rounded to give a softer effect.

Once a shape has been created, it can be filled with various shadings or patterns. Shadings are usually measured in percentages (shades of grey) between white and black. The lower the percentage, the lighter the grey.

Wrapping is where text and graphics meet. Wrapping text around a picture means that one edge of the text will follow the contours of the image. The effect is of the text being displaced to the side. Fitting text to images can be used to give a very sophisticated and professional effect.

D7. Image Control, Back, Front and Transparent

In building up a complete page with Drawn graphics and text, it is important to ensure that different elements mix properly. In building up an image, you will need to hide certain elements in part.

For example, if you were illustrating the inside of a machine, you might want to show it as a 'cutaway' i.e. a drawing of the outside with part of the inside mechanism showing through. This can only be done with proper control of which graphic element is on top of the others.

If a logo consisted of a triangle on top of a circle, you would not want to see the whole of the circle showing through, only a part of it. Thus, sending the circle to the back of the layers will hide the unwanted parts.

However, if you wanted both the circle and the triangle to be seen together, you would need to make both shapes transparent.

Chapter 4. Devising a Value-For-Money D.T.P. System

A. Defining Your Needs

A1. Do You Really Need D. T. P. ?   61

Alternatives
How Do You Decide ?
Trying Out Someone Else's System First

A2. Home, Business, Social or Mixed Use   62

Different Strokes for Different Folks
The Quality and Speed Factors
Overkill or Underkill

A3. D. T. P. versus Word-Processors   62

Features of Modern Word-Processors
Text-Processors and Text Editors
Flexibility versus Simplicity
Text-Handling and Image-Handling

A4. Absolute Necessities, Desires and Costs 63

Needs Determine Necessities
Making a List
Costs of Improvements
Looking to the Future

B. Starting From Scratch

B1. The Basic Computer   66

Which Generation of Processor ?
Upgradeable Chips ?
Which Computer Manufacturer ?
Price, Quality and After-Sales Service
How many Slots and Ports ?

B2. The Floppy and Hard Disks   67

3.5" or 5.25" Floppies ?
MFM, IDE, ESDI or SCSI Hard Disk ?
Cacheing Hard-Disk Controllers

B3. The Internal Memory   68

The Optimum Amount of R.A.M.
Which Type of R.A.M. ?

B4. *The Printer*   *70*

Which Dot-Matrix ?
Which Bubble- or Ink-Jet ?
Which Laser ?
Ordinary Laser or PostScript ?

B5. *The Screen*   *71*

Which Format or Standard ?
Monochrome or Colour ?
Which Size of Screen ?
The Screen Controller Card

B7. *Where and How to Buy*   *73*

Sources of Advice
Complete Systems versus Components
Shops, Mail-Order and Second-Hand
Your Legal Rights
Cash, Cheque, Charge Card or Credit Card

C. *Upgrading an Existing System*

C1. *The Basic Computer*   *75*

Changing the MotherBoard and Processor
OverDrive and Doubler Chips

C2. *The Floppy and Hard Disks*   *75*

From 5.25" to 3.5" Floppies
The New Floptical Drives
A Bigger and Better Hard Disk
Installing A Hard Disk Cache Card

C3. *The Internal Memory*   *76*

Matching and Installing
The Optimum Amount

C4. *The Printer*   *77*

From Dot-Matrix to Bubble-Jet
From Bubble-Jet to Laser
From Laser to PostScript

C5. *The Screen*   *78*

Which Format or Standard ?
Monochrome or Colour ?
Which Size of Screen ?
The Screen Controller Card

C6. *Carrying Out The Upgrade*   *78*

D-I-Y versus Services
Dangers and Warranties

A.   Defining Your Needs

A1. Do You Really Need D.T.P. ?

Alternatives

With photocopiers and word-processors found almost everywhere these days, you can make a more than passable effort by combining these with scissors, paste, time and patience. People have been doing this for years and getting away with it. Stencils and transfers can provide banners and headlines.

Alternatively, if your budget allows, you could get someone else to do the publishing. However, this removes the challenge and the fun of d-i-y.

How Do You Decide ?

Starting from scratch, setting up even the most basic DTP system will cost the best part of £500-£1,000; not cheap by any standards. If you make a mistake and find you are not suited to DTP or it is not what you need, you will have wasted an awful lot of money.

Fortunately, there are strategies that will help you avoid these costly mistakes.

Trying Out Someone Else's System First

The most obvious way is to use someone else's system first before you buy. The system may not be exactly what you would need or would purchase but it will give you an introduction to the complex but rewarding world of publishing. A friend or relative with a system is ideal.

Failing that, a night course at a local tech is probably even better although you may be put off if others around you are more familiar or learn faster. Do not be put off. You are there for your purposes, not theirs. Most other pupils will be at the same level as you.

Computer clubs are also useful if they have equipment for people to try out. Beware of the techno-bores and the one-solution junky ('my system does everything you could ask of it! ') types. Take a cross-section of opinions before deciding how to proceed.

As a last resort, go to a computer shop, preferably when it is quiet and use the equipment. Ignore the sales pitches and don't buy on the spot. Go home and sleep on it'

A2. *Home, Business, Social or Mixed Use*

Different Strokes for Different Folks

When taking advice from other people, remember that your need may not be the same as theirs. If you can find someone in the same position then their experiences could be invaluable.

If you are a member of a club and want to produce a member's newsletter, find someone doing the same thing. You'll probably find they are only too delighted to share their knowledge with you

The most important point is that you decide clearly what you are looking for before you buy. You must first determine if your usage is for home, business, social purposes or a combination of these.

For home use, i.e., the sheer pleasure of achieving a good result can be the most important thing. Few others see the final output so a fairly basic system will suffice. For social purposes, most people would want something better as others will see it and we all like to impress.

In business, the right impression is paramount. Your livelihood and reputation can depend on what others thinks of your efforts.

The level of equipment and quality to aim for is hardest to determine when you have mixed needs. The usual answer is to go for the best you can afford, even if this is overkill in other uses.

The Quality and Speed Factors

These are the distinguishing points of each type of use. Home and pleasure users do not necessarily need either high quality or speed. Also, the coffee machine is usually close at hand. A very limited system comprising of a slow PC, dot-matrix and limited storage often suffices.

For social use, it is better to go slightly higher up-market in terms of speed of computer, printing quality and storage capacity as the demands and deadlines are often much greater. However, if members of a club do not receive a letter currently or is merely typed and copied, they are likely to be impressed by even the most basic modern DTP system. A middle-strength PC, bubble-jet printer and above-average disk size should be sufficient.

In business, the maxim should be, 'Buy the best you can afford'. However, it is also essential that you buy a system that works.

Often business users are tempted to buy something that is technically better specified but do not appreciate that often small gains in quality are sometimes at the expense of ease of use.

For an established business seeking to give a good impression, the minimum specification nowadays is a later generation PC for speed and flexibility, a laser printer and a large hard-disk. A scanner and specialist graphics packages should also be considered.

One of the consequences of rapidly plunging PC prices is that such a system need not cost more than 2-3 times as much as the most basic.

A good business system is likely to cost between £1,000 and £2,000 for the foreseeable future. Soon the laser printer will be more expensive than a decent P.C.

Overkill or Underkill

One of the hardest parts of setting up a system is to know when to stop. Underkill leads to low quality and overkill is a waste of money. The advice below should help you avoid either pitfall.

A3. D. T. P. versus Word-Processors

How About a Word-Processor ?

One of the first question to ask yourself is whether a good word-processor will suit your needs. WP and DTP packages do have similarities though they are important differences to bear in mind.

Anyone who has used a word-processor might be tempted to think that DTP is simply a more powerful version of WP. Some top-end WP's now claim to have DTP incorporated. Don't let advertising hype fool you.

Text-Processors and Text Editors

Text processors and editors, on the other hand, are aimed purely at the entry and printing of text. They have none of the more advanced features and are nowadays mainly used by programmers. In the late Seventies, however, they would have been considered fully-fledged WPs.

Text-Handling and Image-Handling

Real DTP is totally different to WP. With recent WP packages you can type in your text and then format it, add in graphics and charts etc., and make a document look good and professional.

However, the text is still the prime concern. Page layout is constrained by this and it reduces the overall flexibility of design. For straightforward documents, with little design content, this can be perfectly adequate. Company reports needed financial data are a good example.

DTP, on the other hand, looks at both text and graphics as equal. Both can be modified extensively and positioned on the page precisely as you want. The design constraints are far less. You can combine text and graphics in far more ways.

Flexibility versus Simplicity

The aim of this flexibility is to allow creative freedom. This allows you to design much more effective and eye-catching documents. For this reason, DTP's main area of use is in advertising. Even the best WPs do not allow such freedom. However, the user does have to think more and make more decisions. It is very easy to use this freedom inappropriately.

Features of Modern Word-Processors

Modem WPs can use different fonts and type styles, incorporate columns, table, graphs and graphics. For many tasks, they are far quicker than DTP packages. They are still best for letters, circulars and even large reports. Copy typists will certainly appreciate their speed compared to that of an average DTP program.

Probably the best advice is that if your need is mainly for text with just a few other items thrown in then stick to a word-processor. If you want to manipulate the final image to a much higher degree, however, you need DTP.

A4. Absolute Necessities, Desires and Costs

Needs Determine Necessities

For desktop publishing. you have five essential ingredients. A PC-compatible computer, a software package, a hard disk, a suitable monitor or screen, and a printer. The last three can be dispensed with in theory but in practice the benefits are too great.

Making a List

Putting your needs down in black-and-white forces you to think through what you really need. the first list to make is one of all the situations where you might use DTP. Then go back and put a line through all the ones where the advantage is too small to be worthwhile.

Opposite this list, make two columns; Speed and Quality. For each probable use, write whether high speed is essential or low speed will be enough. Then list whether high quality is essential or otherwise.

These lists will now tell you several things. Firstly, they tell whether there are important circumstances when high speed or quality is crucial or whether a basic system is good enough in all cases. Secondly, comparing the cost of an adequate system to your budget, tells you whether you can afford the system you need.

If you cannot then you will end up with an unsuitable system. Such underkill is a waste of money and you would be best advised finding an alternative means of producing printed material or scrapping it altogether. On the other hand, you might find that your needs are much lower than the system you had in mind. This overkill also wastes money.

Costs of Improvements

Of course, you can start with a basic system and build upon it. However, these costs can often be uneconomic when compared with buying something better in the first place. For example, upgrading a first-generation PC to a fourth-generation one is technically possible, but for the cost, you might now be better off just buying a completely new and up-to-date machine.

Looking to the Future

Having made your list of current and identifiable needs, it is worth doing a similar list for future needs. Again, write down as many as you can and then remove any that subsequently appear over-ambitious or unlikely to occur.

If you can identify needs that will soon outstrip the ability of a basic system then you are better off waiting until you can afford the system that will cope with both the present and the future.

B. Starting From Scratch

B1. The Basic Computer

There are many factors influencing the performance of a PC in terms of reliability, expandability and speed. The most important of these is which generation and variation of processor is used. This is followed closely by the 'clock' (or operating) speed of the chip. Other factors to be considered are the future upgrading of the chip, the manufacturer's reputation and the physical layout of the computer box.

Which Generation of Processor ?

The four generations of Intel PC chip, the 8086, 80286, 80386, and 80486, all have many things in common but also have many differences. The first one is extremely limited and, while a few DTP packages will run on such machines, they have very little power. The caffeine factor is extremely high.

The next generation should be considered the minimum level for DTP and even this will involve long waits. The last two are much better suited to the task. Each comes in two flavours; the full 80386 and 80486's called DX and stripped down versions known as SX. The difference between an 80386DX and an 80486SX is minimal.

Therefore there are three machine types to be seriously considered; the 80286 for pure home use, the 80386SX for social and limited business use, and the 80486DX for full business use.

Upgradeable Chips ?

Some recent computers now claim to be upgradeable, i.e., you simply swap your old chip for a nice new one with go-faster stripes. However, this is not recom-mended for the beginner to do on their own. Get a professional to do the removal and replacement.

Which Computer Manufacturer ?

This is a tricky and touchy subject. If you want peace-of-mind then stick to a big-name manufacturer which has a genuine reputation for quality. Don't take the compa-ny's own word for it; read a few magazine with compre-hensive tests or reviews of a manufacturer's full range. One good model doesn't mean they all are.

Choosing a low-priced manufacturer is a different kettle of fish. Some extremely cheap computer firm still manage to give a good level of service and their designs are often ahead of the big-name firms. Look for reviews in magazines that are headlined something like '486's for under £1,000' or 'Budget 386's Head-to-Head'.

Price, Quality and After-Sales Service

As stated above, price and quality do not automatically go hand-in-hand but most people are constrained in their budget. Even so, they must still take into account how much 'support' they will need in terms of advice, repairs and access to staff. The less experienced you are, the more you will need advice.

Choosing a good supplier is difficult for beginners. One strategy is to visit a number of local dealers and go for the one who confused you the least but charged a reasonable price. Never buy on the spot. Go and think about it.

A reputable supplier should also tell you the name of others locally who use their equipment. Ring them up, especially ones with large numbers of machines. Keep your questions short and to the point. Ask simply if they would recommend the firm to a beginner and for DTP.

How many Slots and Ports ?

An important point, often overlooked, is how many slots and ports you might need. Slots allow you to plug-in cards that control other pieces of equipment such as scanners, networks and tape-streamers. If your needs now and in the future are basic then this is not important but ask that there are at least two spare slots just in case.

Ports allow you to communicate with other types of equipment such as printers, modems and mice. Do not buy any system that does not have two serial (mouse and modem) and one parallel (printer) port.

B2. The Floppy and Hard Disks

Disks are essential for storing both programs and data such as document files. Few computer are sold nowadays with only one or two floppies. Hard disks are vastly larger and a standard fixture rather than an optional extra. Don't buy a PC for DTP without a HD!

3..5" or 5.25" Floppies ?

5.25" disks used to be the standard size but they are vulnerable to dust and damage. They also have lower storage capacities and are now an optional extra. However, they are worth considering as they allow you to use text etc. prepared by others with older PCs.

3.5" floppies are encased in a hard plastic sleeve which protects them much better. They can be slipped into a pocket as they are and run little risk of damage. Do not buy a PC without this type of floppy no matter what your needs now and in the future.

MFM, IDE, ESDI or SCSI Hard Disk ?

As regards hard disks, there are a number of different formats. MFM (or RLL) are found on older machines and are slow and relatively low capacity.

ESDI are far more powerful version of MFM but failed to make it in the market and have consequently been phased out by manufacturers.

SCSI disks are very fast and can be very large but are unnecessary for all but the most heavyweight DTP operations. The controller cards are equally expensive.

IDE disks are the ones to choose. They need no special controller card in most computers and are fast and potentially large. As the standard PC hard disk, they sell in sufficient volumes to be reasonably priced. As a simple rule of thumb, expect to pay just over £1 per Mb.

Size of Hard Disk

Size can be important in DTP. If your needs are basic then a 20-40 Megabyte (million items of information) will do for home and social use. For business, however, it is best to invest in a disk of at least 60Mb and preferably over 100Mb. The difference in price is quite small now.

B3. The Internal Memory

Internal memory, known as 'Random Access Memory' or RAM is very fast compare to disk storage but is much more expensive and loses its contents when switched off. It is priced at around £20-30 per Mb but the larger the capacity of the module. the cheaper it is.

The Optimum Amount of R.A.M.

The amount you buy will probably depend on your budget but the rule for any software using large graphics file and screen manipulation is the more the merrier. 2Mb should be considered the practical (but not absolute) minimum. Anything less slows the operation significantly. Less memory, more caffeine.

However, it is easy to go overboard with memory. 4Mb is preferable and 8Mb is considered the optimum. Any more than this and the increase in power is too small to be of value. 4Mb is most cost-effective for normal use.

Which Type of R.A.M. ?

There are several different type of RAM and speeds also vary. Very old systems use memory plugged directly into the main board. This is not to be recommended if you feel you will need to expand later. The risk of damage is high .

Older machines may have memory expansion cards into which you plug the extra chips. This is better as there is little risk of damage to the main board but individual chips may easily be ruined by incorrect insertion as the pins are very thin and fragile.

Some older computers use memory chips mounted on 'Single In-line Plug-in' boards. Whilst they have up to nine chips on a board (2cm by 7cm approx.), they still have fragile pins. However, they are generally better.

Even better are 'Single In-line Memory Modules' or Simms. These are similar to Sips but have thick 'edge connectors' that can only be damaged by repeated removal and insertion scraping the contact off. Most Simms have nine chips on them but the latest only three.

The speed factor is measured in nanoseconds or 'ns'. These are billionths of a second. Slow memory is rated at around 100ns! . Faster ones up to 60ns can be bought but it is crucial that all memory (original or added later) operates at the same speed.

Memory chips can be bought in sizes of 128Kb, 256Kb, 512Kb. 1Mb and 4Mb. Older machines will only accept the first three and have low maximum capacities of 1Mb (an expansion card can be used) but all third and fourth generation computers should accept the latter. Capacities should be at least 16Mb and maybe up to 64Mb.

B4. The Printer

Printers are at least as important as the PC and software you purchase. Making the wrong purchase can be frustrating when what you see on the screen won't appear on the printer. The first and most important tip is; Do not buy a daisy-wheel or golf-ball printer. They won't work. The second is; buy the best printer you can afford. thirdly, buy a printer that uses the Parallel port and not the Serial port. They are much simpler to set up.

Which Dot-Matrix ?

The minimum for DTP is a dot-matrix printer. This uses tiny pins pressing into an inky ribbon to form characters and graphics. They are fast but quality is only passable. Two main types are available; 9-pin and 24-pin. The latter is far better and the difference in price minimal.

Which Bubble- or Ink-Jet ?

A much better alternative is the Bubble-Jet or Ink-Jet printer that uses tubes to blow tiny dots onto the paper. They are much finer than Dot-matrix ones and the resolution far higher. The quality is remarkable and they can be cheaper than many dot-matrix printers.

A good Bubble-Jet is better than an Ink-Jet. The latter suffers from fuzziness on poor quality paper. Some Bubble-Jets produced results virtually indistinguishable from good quality laser printers. They only cost a fraction of the amount and so can definitely be recom-mended for a budget DTP system.

Which Laser ?

If you do have the money then a laser is worth buying on the grounds that they are faster overall and much more robust although the toner cartridges are a hefty price (£25-60). They will print 300 dots-per-inch which gives very good results and can print even fine lines pretty well.

One point to note; if you are going to print out large graphics regularly, it is worth buying a laser with at least 2Mb of RAM built-in. This is because they work by forming a page in memory to start with and then churning it out. If there is not enough memory then the caffeine factor will go through the roof.

Think of a laser as a printer with a computer built-in; the more memory the better it performs.

The other point about memory is that a printer rated at 4 pages per minute (ppm) will only run that fast with multiple copies of the same page. New pages can take ages to formulate.

Their robustness means they are often worth buying second-hand but look inside for signs of dirt and wear. It is also best to avoid very early lasers. Second-generation or MKIIs are the best bet.

Ordinary Laser or PostScript ?

Whenever you read article about DTP, they will usually mention 'PostScript' at some stage. This is system whereby the computer 'describes' each page to the printer. Text is sent as 'formulae' rather than dot-by-dot. This means the files are smaller and faster to send and the fonts can be scaled to virtually any size.

This flexibility is worth having if you are ambitious. However, the price is usually much higher. A good compromise is a second-hand Hewlett-Packard LaserJet II with a JetScript PostScript (<£100) added in. This is not for the beginner to do. Get someone with knowledge to do it as you have to add boards into PC and laser.

B5. The Screen

When you become hooked on DTP (as you surely will) you shall spend many happy hours staring into a screen. This can be very tiring on the eyes.

The two main reason for this screen fatigue are poor definition making characters harder to distinguish and flicker. The latter is caused when the screen is not 'refreshed' (or re-transmitted) often enough. The best screens operate at up to 70MHz (the higher the better). '

Non-interlaced' monitors are far better than interlaced. The most modern screens conform to the MPR II standard. This means that they pump out far less radiation. Although the debate over what harm the radiation can do rages on back and forth, there is no sense in taking chances and the extra cost is now minimal. Pregnant women are especially advised to use low-rad screens.

When choosing a screen, however, it is important to remember that you must also buy a graphics card to go with it. These usually have different combination of resolutions and colour and can greatly affect speeds.

Which Format or Standard ?

Choosing a monitor and card can be highly confusing. The oldest ones are monochrome; colour only came in many years later although even first-generation machines (still produced today) can run colour.

Screen definition was very low as measured in 'Pixels' or dots on the screen. Early models supported only 320 pixels across by 200 pixels down and only a handful of colours. The latest ones can handle up to 1,024 by 756 pixels at thousands (or millions) of colours. Some look more realistic than real life!

For a budget system, aim for at least 640 by 480 and sixteen colours. This standard is known as VGA (or 'Video Graphics Array). Above this is now S-VGA (Super-VGA) which can handle 800 by 600 and 256 colours. Some PC makers consider S-VGA to be 1.024 by 756 and 32,000 colours as mentioned above. It is worth paying attention to screen specification.

Monochrome or Colour ?

Nowadays, it is hardly worth buying a mono screen as the extra hundred or so pounds is well worth spending. Colour allows you to see different parts of the screen stand out better even if, like EPDos2.0, your DTP package does not handle colour. Screen resolutions are also usually higher.

What Size of Screen ?

Many people argue that the bigger the screen the better for DTP. This is generally true but ignores factors such as space and cost Any size up to 14" is reasonably priced at the moment. However, each inch above this adds hundreds to the price. For a budget system, therefore, 14" is the best compromise for size and price.

The Screen Controller Card

The choice of graphics cards is bewildering. Every manufacturer claims theirs is the greatest thing since sliced bread. Many claim performances that only apply in the least demanding circumstances (not DTP). The cards change so fast that it is hard to know what to do.

For the most up-to-date information, the computer magazines' head-to-head tests are best. Look for above-average performance on DTP screen re-draw tests and reviewers' recommendations.

B6. Where and How to Buy

This is another complex and confusing situation the DTP-novice must confront. The risk is wasting a lot of money on a system that will not do what you want. Worse, the equipment may not work or the even not arrive at all. This can be enough to put you off computers for life. Fortunately, you can take precautions.

Sources of Advice

The best advice still remains to try out a someone else's system that meets your requirements adequately. If they are happy with it then you will feel reassured. Beware that not everyone will admit to buying a pig-in-a-poke. Always ask if they would buy the same again with their own money. If they wouldn't then look elsewhere.

You could always hire a computer consultant to advise you but this is expensive and against the spirit of a budget DTP system. The computer magazines offer the best advice around. If you don't understand the jargon then skip to the end of the article and read the verdict or editor's choice section. They usually have a budget one.

Complete Systems versus Components

The components that make up a complete system are notorious for not being fully-compatible with each other. Therefore, it is often reassuring to buy a complete DTP package comprising PC, DTP software and printer.

Unfortunately, these are often made to conform to a particular price for marketing reasons. Compromises are made. Never believe any salesman who says 'you don't really need a bubble-jet or laser for good quality'. Make up you mind about the kind of quality you want and don't settle for anything less.

If you buy each component separately you may still be able to get everything from one supplier. In this case, ask to see it working and get it in writing that everything is compatible with everything else. Put your order in writing. If your order is accepted then a contract has been made and if any incompatibilities arise they are liable.

Buying separately. the best value DTP system would comprise of an 80386SX (16-25MHz), EPDOS v2.0, MS-DOS v5.0, mouse, 3.5"floppy disk, 65-105Mb hard disk, 4Mb Ram, 14" VGA monitor and card, plus a bubble- jet printer. Expect to pay less than £1,000.

Shops, Mail-Order and Second-Hand

Local shops are excellent places to buy from and the human face can be reassuring unless it is some spotty herbert know-nothing just out of school or some mega-whizzkid talking in a foreign language. If you don't understand what they are telling you then buy elsewhere. Never buy on the spot. Go away and think about it.

Look in the magazines for reviews on what the firm has recommended. Always ask what their repairs and spare service is like. Bear in mind that some one-man repair outfits are better than many big firms and expensive service contracts. Prices usually reflect overheads.

Mail-order or 'Direct' buying is increasingly popular and prices are very competitive. However, these companies are not geared to the novice PC user. They send the equipment out and expect the customer to install it If things go wrong, your phone bill can be horrendous.

Your Legal Rights

Everybody has statutory rights no matter what they buy at whatever price (with the exception of purchases from a private individual). You should receive reasonable warranty and the seller is obliged to deliver only 'goods of merchantable quality', i.e., it works.

However, if you simply specify you want a DTP system then this is open to a wide interpretation. If the system does not perform to your expectations then you are left out on a limb. Putting it in writing can be a two-edged sword. If you can, specify the hardware but also add phrases such as 'capable of full page graphics in less than two minutes' or similar. Remember to specify that all components must be compatible.

Cash, Cheque, Charge Card or Credit Card

Payment methods can also affect your rights. If you pay cash, and the firm goes bust or does a runner, don't expect to see your money again. The same applies to a cheque. Credit cards are useful as the credit card company effectively insures your goods whilst the warranty lasts.

If you have problems and the firms is bust they must pay up. However, check the precise terms with your own credit card issuer. Charge cards do not normally carry the same insurance. The best advice is to pay by credit card and settle the amount immediately.

C. Upgrading an Existing System

C1. The Basic Computer

Upgrading generally means you must take out a component and add in a complete replacement. The exceptions are adding more memory and a 3.5" floppy disk. In many cases, the component replaced has little value as you have probably kept it a good while, used it heavily and prices have fallen for new goods. However, you still might be added to recoup some cost by selling the old part second-hand through one of the free-advert magazines.

Changing the MotherBoard and Processor

For older computers, the best way to improve perform-ance without junking the system box is to have the whole motherboard changed. This is reasonably competitive with buying a new machine but you should always use a firm that does board upgrades as a speciality. It can be a tricky job and novices should never attempt it.

It is rarely possible in older machine to change only the chips although some 80286 machine do have an add-in processor card as do some 80386. Unfortunately, though the new chip may be, say, five times more powerful than the old, the motherboard still runs at the design speed and this can constrict performance. The weakest link still determines overall power.

OverDrive and Doubler Chips

Some 80386 and 80486 machines can take advantage of OverDrive or Clock-Doubler chips. These directly re-place the chip and are designed to optimise perform-ance despite the fact that the motherboard is not change. Intel, who make the chips, have lists of which machines can benefit from which chip.

C2. The Floppy and Hard Disks

From 5.25" to 3.5"

Floppies If you have a very old machine that came only with 5.25" floppy disks (probably 360Kb capacity), you can either install the 1.2Mb version or add in the better 3.25" drives. These hold 1.44" and are much safer and are now the standard form of floppy as software producers release all new material on these. 5.25" versions often have to be ordered specially. More powerful software may not even be available in this format.

A Bigger and Better Hard Disk

Assuming you have a hard disk (if you don't then get one), the best way to upgrade it is to add another if possible. Hard-cards are ideal if you just need that little extra. For serious upgrades you will need a separate drive and controller card. If you have an IDE, SCSI or ESDI drive already then you may have a connector for a second hard disk already.

For many systems though, especially older ones and slimline cases PCs, the only real alternatives may be to remove the old one and add a new one. With MFM and RLL you are limited in size. Again, you may need both a new drive and card. Try to replace with an IDE drive of at least 65Mb capacity and preferably over 100Mb. a 200Mb disk is already below the £300 level.

Installing A Hard Disk Cache Card

If you find that, even with a larger disk, you are waiting for the disk to store and retrieve DTP files, you may need to invest in a Cacheing controller. This has RAM on it that temporarily store the data most transferred between PC and disk. It holds this until either is free and it can write or read the data. However, these are not cheap.

C3. The Internal Memory

Matching and Installing

When increasing memory, you must find out precisely which type your machine uses and fit the same again. With older PCs you may need to slot in an additional card which holds the RAM chips.

Newer boards will accept memory modules on the main board but find out exactly what specification you require in terms of speed, size and connection type. You cannot mix and match memory. Your PC manual should tell you which slots to fill. This is important as it can affect performance. For example, if you upgrade from 4Mb to 8Mb, it is best to add in four IMb modules in the next available slots than one 4Mb module anywhere.

The Optimum Amount

RAM should be increased to between 4Mb and 8Mb for DTP. Older machines may be limited to much less than this, in which case, go to the maximum.

C4. *The Printer*

From Dot-Matrix to Bubble-Jet

If you have a dot-matrix printer at the moment, you would be well-advised to upgrade to a bubble-jet (make sure it is a bubble-jet rather than ink-jet). This will enhance the quality of your output tremendously. For £200-300, there are some impressive models around.

You can also put a sheet-feeder on to hold about 50 sheets which is useful if you are printing many copies of each page or one long document. They are not tremendously fast compared to dot-matrices but they fare reasonably well compared with lasers.

Bubble-jets are the leaders in the value-for-money stakes.

From Bubble-Jet to Laser

If money is less of a problem, upgrade to a laser. Make sure it is at least Hewlett-Packard compatible. Remember that toner cartridges will cost between £35-65 but these will print several thousand copies. You must also have enough working space for what amounts to a small photocopier. A second-hand one is useful if you have a large number of copies to print out regularly. A bubble-jet may not take the hammer or hold enough sheets.

The most flexible and cost-effective laser printer has to be the Hewlett-Packard LaserJet II (not IIp or Plus). This has slots for extra memory, PostScript upgrade cartridges and special interfaces. As these are no longer made, you should expect to pick one up for between £400-600 depending upon age and usage. Worthwhile.

From Laser to PostScript

Buying a laser with built-in PostScript can be expensive. Most people would buy one with extra slots to add a cartridge in. If you buy a Hewlett-Packard LaserJet II you can probably find a QMS JetScript upgrade very cheaply but it does require some installation skills.

However, if you do want the enhanced quality and flexibility of PostScript at a reasonable price then this is a recommended upgrade path. Even if you upgrade your DTP software, the above combo should handle it.

C5. The Screen (or Monitor)

Which Format or Standard ?

There is no doubt that if you are upgrading then you should go for a VGA model. This is far better than any of the other standards supported by EPDos. If you want to buy a model that will last for the foreseeable future (and allow for EPDos updates) then buy an S-VGA. EPDos v2.0 will change the screen to VGA automatically.

Monochrome or Colour ?

No contest. Upgrade to colour.

Which Size of Screen ?

Upgrade to a minimum of 12" and preferably go for the 14" models. These are now standard and excellent value.

The Screen Controller Card

Go for an S-VGA card offering 16 colours at VGA standard as this will last you a good while.

C6. Carrying Out The Upgrade

D-I-Y versus Services

Unless you know more than a little about the innards of a PC, find one of the companies that specialise in upgrading as they will have both the parts and the expertise to carry out a safe upgrade.

However, first do your sums to make sure that the cost of the upgrade does not exceed the price of a new machine to your specification. For example, if you want to upgrade from an 8086 to an 80386 SX, you might be better off selling the old one and buying brand new. The different in price may be quite small. It may even be cheaper than upgrading internally

Dangers and Warranties

Messing with the insides of a machine can be dangerous. Never make any changes unless the PC is completely unplugged from any mains power source. That goes for the monitor as well.

Also be careful not to touch the metal edge connectors found on boards. They are highly susceptible to dirt and damage. Chips are very easy to damage. Many components come in anti-static bags. If you remove them from the PC, make sure you return them to the original bag.

Chapter 5.   Setting Up Express Publisher for Dos v2.0

A. Hardware Requirements

A1. The Minimum Needed   80

Processor
Memory
Hard Disk
Screen
Mouse
Printer
Dos Version

A2. A 'Better' Minimum Requirement   81

Processor
Memory
Hard Disk
Screen
Printer
Dos Version
DR Dos v6.0

B. Installing Express Publisher for Dos

B1. Upgrading from EPDos v1.1   83

Deleting the Old - Alternative Strategies
Deleting the Old - Donig the Dirty

B2. New in v2.0   84

B3. Running the Automatic Setup Program   85

Preparation
Sequence

B4. Modifying an Existing Setup   88

B5. Running Under Windows   88

B6. Technical Support   89

- Problems and Queries

A. Hardware Requirements

A1. The Minimum Needed

EPDos specifies a minimum combination of hardware and software that you must have before you can use it successfully. These are detailed below and should be taken as absolute minimum.

Processor

Any IBM-PC Compatible

EPDos will run with any generation of true IBM PC-Compatible from 8088, 8086, 80286, 80386 to the latest 80486 and the 80586 when it arrives. Go for as recent a generation as possible

Memory

640Kb of RAM Memory Inside

Virtually all PCs arrive with a standard 640Kb of RAM memory although older machines may have less. You may get away with 512Kb but the more memory the better so add in a little if you can.

Hard Disk

At Least 3Mb to Spare

It is one thing having a hard disk with a big enough capacity (the minimum is 10Mb), to run EPDos you must check that at least 3Mb is free to use. In reality you will need a lot more.

Screen

VGA, MCGA, EGA, CGA, Hercules

As you will spend an increasing amount of time at the computer, the screen is very important. EPDos will work with all the formats listed above. However, all are fairly low-resolution by today's Super-Vga standards. Aim for the highest resolution. EPDos will run on higher specification screens but will revert to lower-resolution. There is no specification on size but colour is far better.

Mouse

Microsoft, Logitech, IBM plus

EPDos will work with most of the major types of mouse. These include the Dexxa v3.43, Tandy v6.36, Mouse Systems 5.50, Kensington Expert v1.0, Logitech v3.2, v3.4, and v4.0 as well as the true Microsoft mouse v6.14 and v7.04. If your mouse 'jumps' or does not appear, the device driver is either wrongly installed or missing. If you have a different mouse, such as a Genius Model, there is usually a program that allows the mouse to pretend to be a proper Microsoft rodent.

Printer — Nine-Pin Dot-Matrix

There is no minimum specified but obviously the better the printer the more your hard work will be rewarded. For this reason alone, a nine-pin dot-matrix is the absolute minimum although some thermal printers may give an adequate representation of your efforts.

Dos Version — Version 3.0

EPDos is designed to work with a version of Microsoft's Dos that is marked version 3.0 or higher. If you buy a system with Dos pre-installed (especially second-hand) check first if it has a useable version. If not, you will need to upgrade. This is worthwhile for various reasons.

A2. A 'Better' Minimum Requirement

The above is the absolute minimum to get the system operating but, with it, you would soon find DTP a big turn-off (unless you are a masochist in need of a fix). Therefore, a more sensible minimum is suggested below.

Processor — 286 Running at 12MHz

The difference between generations is tremendously but a 286 running at 12 MHz clock speed will give enough power and expansion capability to see you beyond the initial stages of DTP.

Memory — 1Mb for Speed

1Mb gives you just enough extra ooomphh to make EPDos a really useable system. The package will recognise this 'extended' memory. It will also work with more memory than this that uses the Lotus-Intel-Microsoft standard v4.0 or higher (known as LIM-EMs 4).

Hard Disk — Budget for 40Mb

There are some 10Mb disks around but 20Mb is the standard. However, DTP files become large if they use graphics a lot. In this case, a 40Mb hard disk is much better and anything up to 100Mb is usually good value. Go for an IDE drive if possible.

Screen — VGA is Very Good All-Round

If you don't want to end up squinting and fatigued visually, the VGA screen is the real minimum and preferably one that is non-interlaced and pumps out only a low level of radiation.

Printer

Blow Bubbles

Given the only slight difference in price between a good dot-matrix and a bubble-jet, the latter should be taken as the true minimum as you can really see fineness of your work on the paper. The quality compares with a laser and this is the level of quality that makes DTP worthwhile.

Dos Version

Improving Software Management

Later Dos's are more stable, i.e., they breakdown much less often. They also have more functions and can handle much bigger hard disks. One of the major reasons for upgrading is that later versions, particularly version 5.0 have much better and more sophisticated memory management features. This can speed up the operation of DTP quite a lot.

Bottlenecks in data being sent to and from the hard disk can cause your system to grind to a temporary halt. Better management of the most used data and writing to the disk when the machine is not being used (cacheing) mean that even normally slow machines can appear to speed up.

DR Dos v6.0

An Alternative to Microsoft's Dos

A rival firm called Digital Research generally manages to keep its version of Dos one step ahead of Microsoft's. It offers more features including extremely useful ones such as data compression. This can effectively double the capacity of your hard disk. It is well worth checking out if you are having problems with your setup.

B.   Installing Express Publisher for Dos

B1. Upgrading from EPDos v1.1

Upgrading an old and trusted package can be both heart-rending and heart-stopping. Will I understand the new package? What happens if the new package won't install properly? How do I recover? Who do I ask?

Deleting the Old   Alternative Strategies

The EPDos manual recommends that you delete the any old versions of EPDos before installing the new. Not everyone is that brave. There are two strategies you can employ to get around the problem but you must have enough space on your hard disk to hold the old and the new versions plus the files for both.

The first strategy is to copy all existing files to new directories that will not be used by the new EPDos program. If your old files are in the 'C:\Express' then you should create a new directory and copy all the files. This can be done by using the commands similar to the ones below (they will differ from your system possibly);

```
MKDIR C:\exprold
COPY C:\express\*.* c:\exprold\*.*
```

If you have one or more sub-directories, for example, 'C:\Express\text\', it is worth creating equivalent sub-directories in the new one and copying data across, e.g.,

```
MKDIR C:\exprold\text\*.*
COPYC:\express\text\*.* C:\exprold\text\*.*
```

This can be tedious so a second strategy can be employed instead. When EPDos is installing, it will ask you what directory you want to use. A default name is given of 'C:\Express' but you should type over a new name such as 'C:\epdos2.0'. The installation program will then create this new directory.

However, it has the slight drawback that any examples in the manual using the default directory will, in effect, be inaccurate. You must always bear this in mind, especially if others use your system. Also, should a problem arise, if you need to speak with Technical Support staff you will need to remember the new directory name.

83

Deleting the Old   Doing the Dirty

Once you are sure that no important data is held in the old directory, you need to erase the individual program files that make up EPDos. To make sure you are in the dirctory known as the 'Root' directory, type;

CD\

Then you must switch to the EPDOs directory by using the command;

CD C:\express

You should see the phrase 'C:\EXPRESS>' on the screen if you are in the right directory. If not, start again. You can try typing;

DIR /P

The third line down should state the directory name.

When you do see the phrase 'C:\EXPRESS>', type in the following and cross your fingers etc.;

ERASE ep*.*

All your old EPDos program files should have been wiped clean from the directory so that you can now install the new version using the installation software.

B2. New in v2.0   A Whole Host of New Features

Version 2.0 is a substantially revised EPDos. These make the package more flexible, easier to manipulate and means it is on a more even par with more expensive DTP packages costing a great deal more.

The major innovation is the TextEffect package that is included (mentioned in previous chapters). TE allows you to create 'graphics' from text. For example, if your organisation is called 'Global Widget Distribution' you may want to curve this name around a picture of a globe. Or you might want the text to stand out from the page by giving it one of several '3-d' effects.

The new Text Frame tool allows you to pre-define where text is placed on a page. You draw the rectangle and all the text is placed in this area. Frames can be copied.

To be able to do both fine adjustments and see the overall picture, Zoom In and Out facilities now included allow you to go twice as near or far each time you use them.

Most publications are printed in Portrait format, i.e, taller rather than wider, but now you can print in Landscape or wide format. This is often useful for graphics.

DTP often combines many elements to produce a particular effect. A graphic of a house may be made up of straight lines, circles, rectangles etc. However, if you decided you want to move the whole picture elsewhere on the page, you previously had to move each element in turn. In EPDos2 you can select all the ones you want grouped together and then move them en bloc.

If a publication runs to several pages, you will probably want something to identify the document, where you are on it and number the pages for your own reference and the readers'. The features 'Headers' and 'Footers' now allow you to do this. Page numbering is also automatically updated if you add or delete pages.

Graphic images brought into EPDos in the TIF format can not be cut down or cropped to fit the space reserved in the publication. You can also use graphics held in the CGM format which will greatly increase the amount of artwork you can incorporate from commercial sources.

Certain features, that were included in earlier version as an icon in the Toolbox, are now relegated to menu commands. This is due to the addition of more useful features that are needed regularly. These chages are;

Old Tool	New Command	Menu
Magnify	Edit Bit Image	Objects
Crop	Crop Image	Objects
Send to Front	Send to Front	Objects
Send to Back	Send to Back	Objects

B3. Running the Automatic Setup Program

This part of EPDos has a high caffeine factor so now is the time to make that copy and practice meditation. Fortunately, it is not as bad as some programs but even on an 80486 machine with a high-speed disk, it can still take between ten and twenty minutes to feed in all the necessary files off the four disks.

Preparation

Checking Everything is Okay

there are several things you should do and know before starting to install EPDos to your hard disk. The manual says to check your mouse is working first but this is not easy if you do not have another mousey program.

You will find out soon enough when you first run the package for the first time (if the mouse ever fails to appear, press the 'ALT' key simultaneously with the letter 'F' and then press the 'X' key to exit the program). you will have to check your mouse instructions.

Next, check how much memory you have spare on your hard disk. Type 'DIR' at the 'C:>' prompt to find out. Make sure you have 3Mb at least and 5Mb if you want all the clip art images. If you don't have enough space then do not try to install. Clear some space or get a bigger disk drive.

Also, if you do not know which type of screen you have, try to find out. Fortunately, there is an option for those who cannot find out what they have.

The manual suggests that you must have the statements;

FILES=20
BUFFERS=20

In a file called 'C:\CONFIG.SYS' before you start. If they are not present you need to add them but if you have never done this before, contact either MicroSoft's helpline for Dos or your EPDos distributor to talk you through it. The CONFIG.SYS file is absolutely crucial to your system.

Finally, make sure you have the four disks at hand. Make coffee and start chanting mantras.

Sequence

Following Screen Instructions

Some people prefer to switch their machine off and back on again before installing but this is purely a matter of personal preference. It should make little difference. To ensure you are initially in the Root directory, type;

CD\

Then put Disk 1 in the floppy disk drive (preferably Drive A:) and then type;

A:

The disk drive should start whirring. When 'A:>' appears on the screen, it is time to type;

SETUPEP

This will start the installation program running. A title screen appears briefly before it is replaced with one explaining that files will be copied to the hard disk and the program configured for your hardware. Press the Space Bar when you have read the message.

You will then be asked what type of screen you are using. You can choose from a list by moving up and down it with the cursor key and then pressing the F10 key to indicate you have the right one.

If you do not know what type you have, EPDos can make a 'guess'. if, later, this appears to be wrong (the program screen does not work) you can always try the others until you get it right. Select the 'I don't know' option and press the F10 key to continue.

You will then be shown a list of directories where the installation program proposes to store the EPDos program, documents, art, text files and fonts. If you think they are okay then press F10.

If not, move the cursor down and type your preferred directory name. this option is very useful if you do not wish to override an earlier version of EPDos. Press F10.

Next you are aked whether you wnat to use Inches, Picas or Centimetres. The latter is the easiest to use so move down the list and press F10.

The coffee-drinking session starts here. the installation program has determined your hardware configuration and your wishes. Now, lots of files will be copied from the floppies to the hard disk. Whilst it does this, EPDos shows the file name and a bar indicating how much of each file has been transferred.

You will be asked for Disk 2 so take out Disk 1 and replace it. You can either press ENTER to continue, ESC to exit the installation, or a different disk drive letter. If you enter the wrong disk, the program will tell you to change it.

Disk 2 will simply be copied over so you can take another swig of coffee. It will then ask you to put Disk 3 into the drive before asking you to choose which printers you wish to have installed. Run down the list with the cursor keys and press ENTER for any you want. A small tick-mark will appear beside chosen ones. When you have finished, press F10. You will be asked for Disk 2 again.

If your printer does not appear in the list, you must try to find out what other printers yours can 'emulate' or pretend to be. For example, one bubble-jet printer can also act like an IBM Pro-Printer or an Epson dot-matrix. You will have to look in your printer manual and maybe make changes to the hardware.

Next you are asked if you wish to copy all the high-resolution (300 dots per inch) clip-art to the hard disk. If you press ENTER against the first line on the list then all files will be copied. Otherwise, move up and down the and use ENTER to choose the ones you want. Press F10.

You will now be asked to put Disk 4 in the drive. drink dregs of coffee until the screen says that you have successfully installed EPDos and asks you to press the ENTER key.

You will then be given a list of items installed or configured. This list is also the one you will use when altering the configuration later on. Move the cursor to the last choice and press ENTER to exit the installation program. You should see the 'A:>' prompt.

Congratulations ! You have now installed EPDos2.

B4. Modifying an Existing setup

To modify or re-configure you EPDos system, you should run the SETUPEP program that resides in the C:\EXPRESS directory. You will then be asked which aspects you wish to modify. the process is similar to the one described above for the different parts.

B5. Running Under Windows

If you have Windows on your system, you can run EPDos from it. However, it will not run in a small window, it insists on using the full screen. EPDos should be installed onto Program Manager just like any other Dos program but you must use the '.pif' file rather than the '.com' one.

If you really want to use DTP in Windows, upgrade your EPDos to Express Publisher for Windows (EPWin) as this really uses the advanced features far better. The look and feel is far smoother and more sophisticated and the rough edges have been taken off.

B6. Technical Support - Problems and Queries

Hopefully you will have few problems but even experienced users hit difficulties they cannot solve themselves. This is where the Technical Support lines come in handy.

When things go wrong, quickly write down what you were doing immediately before the trouble. This can be invaluable to the support staff.

Also, try to be sat next to your computer and set it up at the point where you are hitting hassles. Complex procedures are more easily described to you this way and you can be 'talked down' to a safe landing.

Chapter 6.   Starting Express Publisher

A.   Starting the Program   *92*

B.   The Express Publisher Screen

    B1. Icons   *93*
    B2. Pointers   *93*
    B3. Menus   *93*
    B4. Scroll Bars and Thumb   *94*
    B5. Rulers   *95*
    B6. Screen Refresh Button   *96*
    B7. Message Line   *96*
    B8. Keyboard and Shortcuts   *96*
    B9. Dialog Boxes   *96*

C.   Starting a New Document

    C1. Standard   *96*
    C2. Loading a Template   *97*
    C3. Creating a Custom Page   *98*
    C4. Loading an Existing Document   *98*

A. Starting the Program

Starting EPDos is fairly straightforward. When you switch on your computer, you will eventually arrive at the 'C:>' prompt where you need to enter the following commands (remember to press ENTER after each);

Type	CD C:\EXPRESS
Type	EP

The first command changed the directory to the EPDos one and the second is the name of the main program file. If you are not using the hard disk as drive C:, you must substitute the relevant letter in all exercises.

The disk should whirr away for a while until the package is loaded. However, if your disk is too full you will see the following on the screen;

Unable to create working copy

In this case, you will have to delete other files you no longer need (make sure you copy them to floppy first just in case). You should aim to have at least 135 - 300Kb of spare disk space although even this is pushing it given how large graphics files can quickly become.

Assuming all goes well, the EPDos screen will appear as will a small arrow or Pointer. This is controlled by the mouse and it will move when you move the mouse.

B. The Express Publisher Screen

Most of the elements on the EPDos screen were detailed in Chapter 2 so here we will just have a quick play with some of the main features.

B1. Icons

A Toolbox of Fast features

The icons or pictures on the second line of the screen are used to access all the most important features used to design and flesh out a page. Move your mouse and watch the arrow-shaped pointer glide across the screen.

Now move the tip of the pointer to the first icon along and click the left-hand button on the mouse. The icon will change shade or colour to indicate is has registered you wish to activate that feature.

B2. Pointers

Different Pointers, Different Modes

The pointer will change shape depending on the feature you are using. The arrow-head pointer is the normal one and this used to select objects and manipulate them by such things as changing their size. Let's see what other shapes come up.

If you now move the cursor down below the ruler you will see that its shape has not yet changed. However, if you move the pointer to the second icon along , click with the left-button and then move the pointer down again to the working area, you will see it now resembles a fancy letter 'T' with a bar through it. This is known as the 'I-Beam' pointer and indicates you wish to enter or alter text.

If you now do the same with the fourth icon, you will see that the pointer has become a pen. This indicates that you are going to draw a shape on the screen.

Later on you will see another type known as the Four-headed Arrow pointer used for moving objects around.

If you ever do something that takes the machine a while to actually do (a frequent DTP occurrence), you will see a small clock-face appear. This is known as the Watch pointer in the manual but is not truly a pointer. It is best to do nothing while this symbol can be seen. In some circumstances a coffee cup might be more appropriate.

B3. Menus

Essential Features Selector

You might wonder why all features are not represented by icons. The simple truth is that the screen is not big enough, too many would be confusing, and some features cannot be easily represented as a picture. Therefore, the less used features are kept hidden in various menus listed on the top line of the screen.

To reveal the full menu, move the pointer to the word File on this Menu Line and press the left-mouse button (Left Click). A list of twelve features or options should now appear as if by magic. For the moment, do not click any of these options.. That will come later.

B4. Scroll Bars and Thumb

Position on the Page

On the right of the screen you will see a vertical bar with a small square plus up and down arrows. This is a scroll bar. There is another at the bottom of the screen.

These are used to overcome the small size of the screen. A normal sheet of paper is much larger than your screen so you need to move around. Imagine having a camera focused quite close to a newspaper page and moving around. At some stage you will see only the headline and at others the main text of the story.

The squares or 'Thumbs' indicate how far down and across you are on the page (or even off it). At the moment, you should only be able to see a small part of the top of a blank page. Move the pointer to the up-arrow in the top right-hand and Left-Click on it. The screen will 'jump, i.e. you have moved the page up and can now see slightly lower down the page.

Remember; image the screen is connected to a camera close to the page. Later you will see how to have the whole page displayed. Click on the other arrows.

To make bigger jumps, click on the scroll bar itself. If you click above the Thumb, you will move much further down the page. Click below and you will move back up.

Finer movements can be made using the Thumb itself. Move the pointer onto the Thumb and press the left button but do not release it yet (known as left Left-Hold). Now slide the mouse up very slightly and the page will move slightly too. Still holding, move it back down to see the reverse. This is very useful for making precise moves whether working close up or far out from the page.

B5. Rulers

For Fine Positioning

The rulers are marked in the units you choose during installation and there is one on the third line down and on the left-hand side. When you move the mouse and pointer, you will see thin lines move at the same time. This helps you know more precisely where you are.

B6. Screen Refresh Button

Clearing Debris

A tiny little star tucked away in the extreme bottom right-hand corner indicates the Screen Refresh feature. Sometimes, especially when you are changing the objects on screen a lot, you will see that the alterations are not properly shown. There may be a line still showing that has been moved or erase. In this case, simply move the pointer to the Screen Refresh Button and Left-Click. The image on screen will be completely redrawn.

B7. Message Line

The Bottom Line

The bottom line on the screen is used by the EPDos package to give you reminders, indicate the features being used, give guidance, and give warnings of errors. Sometimes the messages will only be displayed for a brief period although this can usually be extended by keeping you finger on the mouse button.

B8. Keyboard and Shortcuts

Text and Commands

The mouse is tremendously useful but there are some times when you just have to start using them ol' fingers. When entering a piece of text there is no alternative.

However, you can also use the keyboard to enter some commands using the 'Function' keys. For example, pressing the key marked 'F3' will move you to the previous page if you have more than one. F4 moves you to the next. These keys can often be quicker than using the mouse and menus if you can remember them.

All menu commands can be entered using the 'Alt' key and pressing the letter underlined. Look at the Menu Line. You will see each menu name has one letter underlined. Press Alt followed by T to display the Text Menu options. To remove the menu, press the key marked 'Esc' (i.e., Escape). This method holds good for all commands and menus. If you mouse ever breaks down it will be a life-saver.

B9. Dialog Boxes

Conversing with EPDos

When you activate certain features, you will see a small box appear known as a Dialog Box (american spelling unfortunately). This allows you to specify your command even further and set different options. For example, Left-Click the Set Line icon (eighth from the left) and a box with different line thicknesses will appear. Point to and Left-click on one before Left-Clicking < OK >.

C. Starting a New Document

C1. Standard   *A Choice of Standard Layouts*

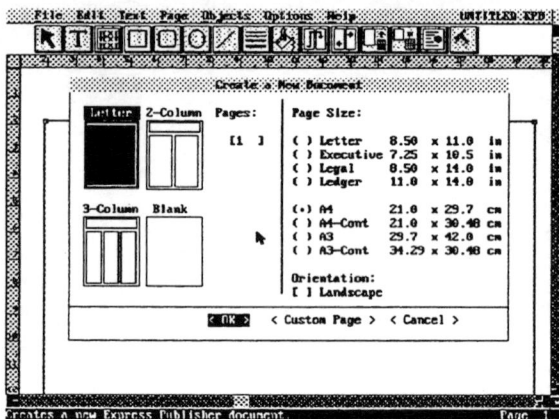

EPDos has a number of pre-defined layouts that you can choose from. To do so;

Left-Click (menu)	File
Left-Click	New
Dialog Box (appears)	'Create a New Document'
Left-Click	( ) A4
Left-Click	3-Column
Left-Click (no. of pages)	1
Type (no. of pages)	2
Left-Click	< OK >

This has opened the File Menu, chosen the New (document) option, set paper to A4 and pages to 2 with a 3-column format. When you click on OK, the screen will change to the following showing how text will flow;

C2. Loading a Template

Templates are different from the type of layout you have just loaded in that it is a layout for a specific purpose. For example, you might be running a newsletter for a society. You could take a basic layout and modify it. then you could put in the name and logo, the contents section, a picture highlight the major story inside etc.

EPDos has a number of these which we can look at like the one below called 'NEWSLTR.EPT'.

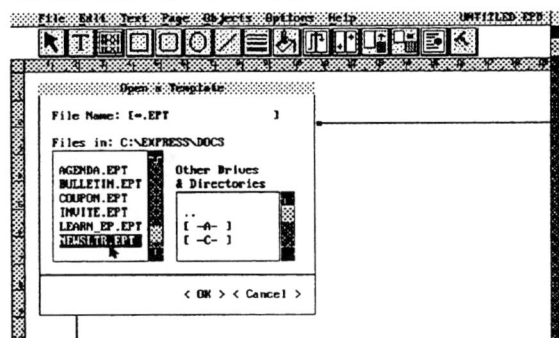

To load this template, do the following;

Left-Click (menu)	File
Left-Click	Open Template
Dialog Box (appears)	'Open a Template'
Left-Click	Newsltr.ept
Left-Click	< OK >
Watch Pointer (appears)	

| Left-Click (menu) | Page |
| Left-Click | Show Page |

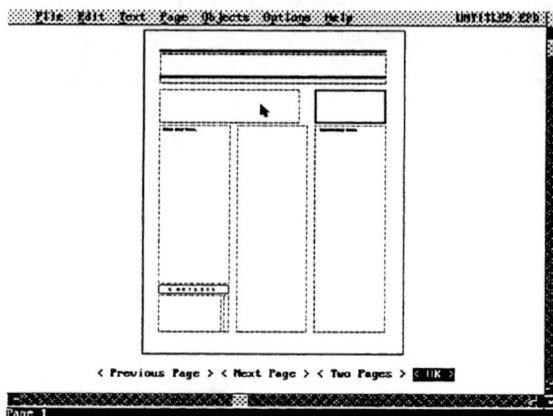

| Left-Click | < OK > |

This will have opened the File menu, chosen the Open Template option, chosen the Newsltr template, shown the front page in actual size and then in full page size.

C3. Creating a Custom Page

If you choose, you can create a page to your own specification by using the New option in the File menu and then clicking on the <Custom Page> choice. However, this is covered in more detail in later chapters.

C4. Loading an Existing Document

The same applies to loading a previously created document using the File Menu and Open options. When you have gone through the various exercises later in this book, you will have saved some work to disk that you can re-open later.

Chapter 7.   Handling Text

A.   Text Frames

A1. Creating a Frame   100
A2. Entering Text   100
A3. Moving with the Cursor Keys   101
A4. Moving with the Mouse   101
A5. Moving the Frame   102
A6. Resizing and Shaping the Frame   102
A7. Text Formatting   103
A8. Adding, Deleting and Editing Text   104
A9. Story Flow - Linking and Unlinking   105
A10. Zooming In and Out   107

B.   Fonts

B1. Determining the Current Font   108
B2. Selecting Text   108
B3. Type Face   109
B4. Type Sizes   110
B5. Type Attributes   110
B6. Changing the Entire Font   111

C.   Text Formatting

C1. Justifying Text   112
C2. Tabulation   112
C3. Hyphenation   115
C4. Text Frame Margins   115
C5. Character Spacing   118
C6. Kerning   119
C7. Line Spacing   120
C8. Paragraph Spacing   121
C9. Paragraph Text Styles   122

A. Text Frames

The use of a frame to act as a boundary to your text is to make things easier. A block of text is kept together and you can create a layout more precisely. The exercises below will show you all the basic facilities associated with text and frame handling.

A1. Creating a Frame

Follow the steps below;

Left-Click

Pen Cursor	(appears)
Bottom Line (reads)	'Select Anchor Point and hold down the mouse button'
Move Mouse	(to top left-hand corner of page)
Left-Hold	(keep button down)
Move Mouse	(down and right until frame 4cm by 10cm seen on screen)
Mouse	(release button)
Frame	(appears as below)

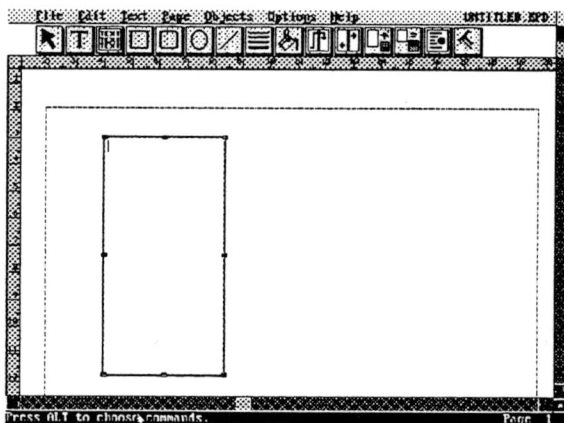

A2. Entering Text

Continue this exercise by doing the following;

Cursor	(flashes in top left of frame)
Type	'This is my first piece of text in Express Publisher for Dos.
	I hope it is good enough to impress my friends when I show them what I can do with a DTP package.

Today DTP, tomorrow the world !
(After I've bought more coffee in).

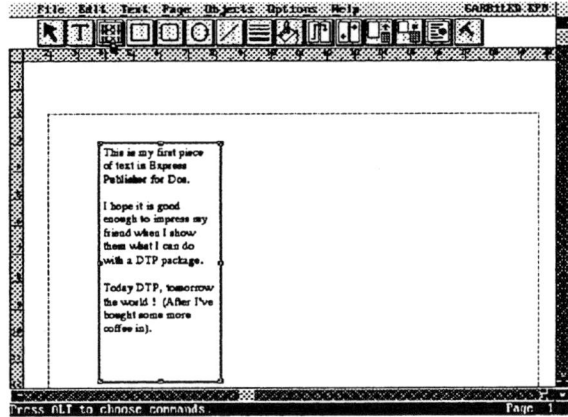

You have now created and sized a text frame and entered three paragraphs of text into it. Remember that normally a paragraph consists of more than one sentence and is ended using the ENTER key.

A3. Moving with the Cursor Keys

Some of the text you have typed may need changing and this can be done in one of two ways. The first is to use the cursor control keys Up, Down, Left and Right (keys with arrows on them on your keyboard).

You are currently at the end of the text in the frame. Suppose we want to add a new sentence at the end of the first paragraph. Use the cursor control keys to position the cursor after the full stop of the second paragraph. Then type; 'I think I will show them this example.'

This new sentence will now be added to the frame and later sentences moved down a little.

A4. Moving with the Mouse

You can also move with the mouse. This is more useful when you have to move over a longer distance. A good example would be an A4 report where each page has only one very large text frame. In this case you would be able to move from the top to the bottom with the mouse much more easily. For this example, however, simply move the mouse pointer over the first letter in the top left of the frame and Left-Click. Now insert a few words.

101

A5. Moving the Frame

The frame you have created may not be in the correct position so we need to know how to move it on the page and on the screen. The pointer is the wrong type at the moment. We need the Arrow-Head Pointer. Move the pointer to the first icon in the Toolbox and Left-Click. You should now see the Arrow-head again.

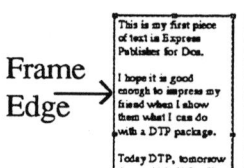

Frame Edge →

> This is my first piece of text in Express Publisher for Dos.
>
> I hope it is good enough to impress my friend when I show them what I can do with a DTP package.
>
> Today DTP, tomorrow

Move Mouse	(until the arrow touches the frame)
Left-Hold	(hold button down)
Move Mouse	(to the right about 5cm)
Mouse	(release button)

You will now see that the whole frame has been moved. This is invaluable when trying to design and test new layouts for newsletters, magazines etc. The screen becomes the canvas or 'paste-board' (a designer's term) upon which you can express your ideas of style etc.

A6. Resizing and Shaping the Frame

You may decide that a frame is the wrong size and shape to fit in the whole text or blend in with the intended design. Fortunately, you can change both size and shape. To do this, you need to move the Frame Handles. These are shown when you;

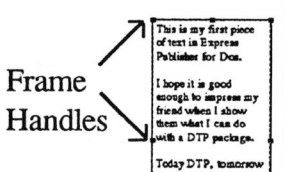

Frame Handles

> This is my first piece of text in Express Publisher for Dos.
>
> I hope it is good enough to impress my friend when I show them what I can do with a DTP package.
>
> Today DTP, tomorrow

Move Mouse	(until arrow-head touches frame edge)
Left-Click	(frame changes)

You will now see the corners of the frame, and half-way down each side, there are small black squares; the handles. By 'Dragging' these, you can change the frame.

Move Mouse	(to top right handle)
Left-Hold	(hold button down)
Move Mouse	(a few cm right and up)
Mouse	(release button)

The frame is now larger and squarer than before. The text has stayed the same size and shape but the paragraphs have become longer and are spread over fewer lines. The left-hand edge of the frame has not changed at all.

You can try the same with the other handles just for fun. If you click the top-middle handle and move it up you will see the frame become longer etc. Note that the corner handles change size and shape in two directions whilst the middle ones only alter in one direction.

102

A7. Text Formatting

Having changed the size and shape of the frame, we can also re-shape the paragraphs and fonts. One of the main features to change is the way the text is spread across the column of text in the frame. This is called 'Alignment' or 'Justification' (in EPDos but not in other packages).

All the text in a frame should run the same way. The current frame is 'Left-Aligned', i.e., the characters are flush to the left-hand side but not to the right.

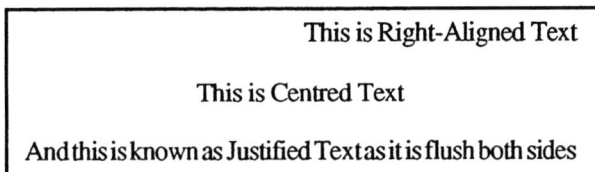

> This is Right-Aligned Text
>
> This is Centred Text
>
> And this is known as Justified Text as it is flush both sides

To change the alignment;

Move Mouse	(over the text frame)
Left-Click	(so frame handles seen)
Move Mouse	(over Text option in Menu Line)
Left-Click	(Text menu appears)
Move Mouse	(over Justify Text option)
Left-Click	(to show Dialog Box)

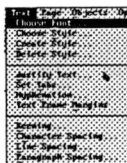

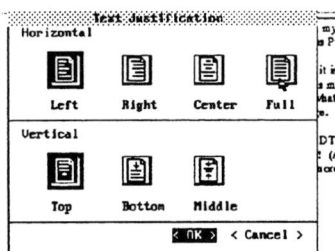

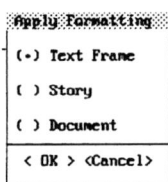

Move Mouse	(to icon marked 'Full')
Left-Click	Full
Left-Click	< OK >
Dialog Box	'Apply Formatting' appears
Left-Click	< OK >

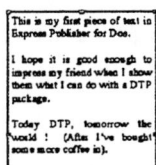

The text will now be flush to both sides of the frame. As you will have seen, there are several other options such as justifying text vertically within a frame. Try a few of these using the same routine as above. You can also apply a particular type of justification to a story spread over a number of frames or over every frame in the whole document. The latter gives a strong 'identity'.

103

A8. Adding, Deleting and Editing Text

You have already seen how to add text in using both the cursor control keys and the mouse. You can also use both of these to delete and enter text. It depends on what you want to do as to which is easier to use.

For small changes near where the text cursor is already positioned nearby, it is usually easier to use the cursor keys. Where you have large blocks to be changed or they are distant from the cursor position, use the mouse.

Move Mouse	(to the second icon in the Toolbox)
Left-Click	Text
Move Mouse	(to last word in last paragraph)
Left-Click	(cursor appears in last word)
Cursor Up	(repeatedly until in last line/first para)
Cursor Right	(until between 's' and full stop)
Type	'and I think it is a very good package'

You will now see that this text has been added or inserted into the original paragraph. Now we will do a similar exercise using the mouse to move around.

Move Mouse	(to after last full stop of last para)
Left-Click	(I-beam cursor now positioned there)
Type	'This is an editing exercise'

You will see the text has been added to the end of the paragraph. You will also note how quick and easy this method is. This is why it is used to edit a whole document or story after the basic text has been entered.

You can also delete text by similar methods. Move the cursor to a particular word and then press the Delete key (which may be marked by either 'Delete', 'Del' or a left-pointing arrow or 'Backspace').

You can also remove more than one character at a time using the mouse. Do the following;

Highlighted Text ⟶

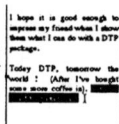

Move Mouse	(to start of 'This is an editing exercise')
Left-Hold	(hold button down)
Move Mouse	(to right - text highlighted)
Move Mouse	(down - to highlight rest of sentence)
Mouse	(release button)
Delete Key	(text will disappear)

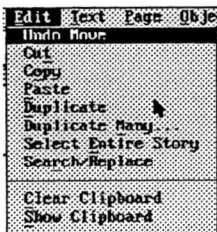

The sentence should have now been removed completely from the frame. However, if you make a cock-up, you can retrieve the text by;

Move Mouse	(to Edit in Menu Line)
Left-Click	Text
Move Mouse	(to Paste option)
Left-Click	(menu disappears)

The text has now been restored as if by magic. Unfortunately though, this only works as long as you have not deleted or 'cut' anything else in the meantime.

Using these techniques above, you would type it all in all the text of a story or document, print it out, inspect it, and make any changes. This process is called 'Editing' if you make substantial changes to the layout, content or style and 'Proof-reading' if you are only checking for grammatical and spelling accuracy.

A9. Story Flow - Linking and Unlinking

Many stories will fill more than one frame; this is especially true when producing a book or in magazines and newspapers that use columns of text. For this reason alone, you need to make sure that text will flow between different frames.

Imagine a story spread over three columns (or frames) and packed full with text. When you are proof-reading, you notice that you have retyped an entire paragraph in the first column. You <u>have</u> to delete it.

Without automatic flowing, you would then need to cut the first part of the second column and transfer it to the end of the first column. You would have to do this for each column.

Automatic flowing cuts this out entirely. By linking each column in a specific sequence, any changes made in one column carry through to the others without you having to do anything. All the cutting and transferring is done for you. This is a god-send when dealing with large stories.

The changes also apply across pages. It is common in newspapers to put the header and a few paragraphs on the front page and then say 'Continued on Page 12' at the end. When you turn to page 12 you find the rest of the story in more detail. This puts the crux of many more important stories on the front page and indicates content.

105

We will now extend the current story to a second frame.

Move Mouse	(to third icon in Toolbox)
Left-Click	
Pen Pointer	(appears)
Move Mouse	(to right of current frame)
Left-Hold	(keep button down)
Move Mouse	(until similar-sized frame appears)
Mouse	(release button)
Move Mouse	(to tenth icon in Toolbox)
Left-Click	
Bottom Line	'Select Source Text Frame'
Link Cursor	(similar to icon will appear)
Move Mouse	(over original frame)
Left-Click	(to indicate this is first paragraph)
Bottom Line	'Select Destination Text Frame'
Move Mouse	(to newly-created frame)

The two frames are now linked together with the original one being first and any new text flowing automatically into the second. To test this out;

Move Mouse	(to second icon in Toolbox)
Left-Click	
Move Mouse	(to end of text in first frame)
Left-Click	(to position text cursor)
Type	(several paragraphs of text)

As you come to the end of the first frame, the cursor will suddenly jump to the new frame and you can continue typing away quite merrily. If you type without looking at the screen you probably won't even notice the jump.

Beware, however, that the new frame may not have the same formatting as the first. This often happens if you have cut text from an entirely different frame and the pasted it into the first one. You may well have to re-format the second frame using the methods demonstrated in section A7 previously. This time, choose the option that allows you to format the whole story or document.

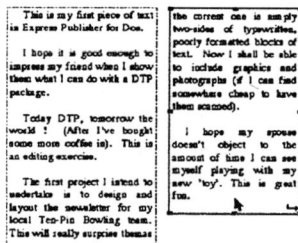

A10. Zooming In and Out

One of the most useful aids to editing is the Zoom feature. You would normally see the current page in 'Actual Size' mode. This means that EPDos is trying to portray the size of print and paper on the screen. It is not always accurate but is a good enough representation for most purposes.

However, fine editing requires a closer view (whether it is text or graphics you want to inspect. Another use is when you are using very small text or if you require glasses (which sometimes can cause problems when looking at computer screens).

To learn how to Zoom In;

Move Mouse	(to Page option Menu Line)
Left-Click	Page
Move Mouse	(to Zoom In option)
Left-Click	Zoom In

The screen will now change and you will see part of the page in a magnification many times actual size. You can move around using the thumb and scroll bars at the bottom and right-hand sides.

Unfortunately, this method of zooming in is rather tedious if you have to do it regularly. An easier and quicker method is to use a keyboard short cut. To zoom in, simply press the SHIFT and F2 keys simultaneously. This works between each level of zoom.

Another short-cut is to use the Arrow-Head pointer to select the object or frame you wish to inspect by Left-Clicking on it and then using SHIFT F2.

The same sequence of commands applies to the Zoom Out feature. What you do is;

Move Mouse	(to Page option on Menu Line)
Left-Click	Page
Move Mouse	(to Zoom Out option)
Left-Click	Zoom Out

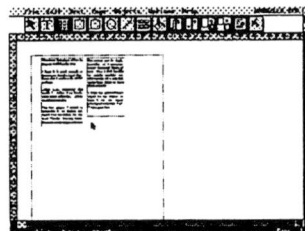

The screen will now change and you will see most of the page in a magnification of many times less than actual. Again, this is rather tedious if you have to do it regularly. A quicker method is to use a keyboard short cut. To zoom out, simply press the F2 key. Experiment !

107

B.   Fonts

Fonts are often crucial to the visual success and legibility of a document. The wrong typeface, size or attributes can make a document look a complete mess. This is one reason why the companies that devise fonts have been able to command such high prices.

Creating a successful and attractive font is also painstaking work carried out by highly-skilled typographic designer. Every curve or line has to be precise and translating these into a language computers can understand and reproduce accurately is very complex

To demonstrate the variety of fonts available, we will now do a short exercise. First, you must create a text frame almost the width of the page and at least six centimetres deep. Then, type 'The cat sat on the mat' five times or more.

B1. Determining The Current Font

Often it is useful to know what a certain font already used is in terms of type face, size and attributes. To do this;

Move Mouse	(to second icon in Toolbox)
Left-Click	
Move Mouse	(to first line of 'The Cat sat on...)
Left-Click	(between two characters)
Move Mouse	(to Text option on Menu Line)
Left-Click	Text
Move Mouse	(to Choose Font option)
Left-Click	Choose Font

Dialog Box   ('Choose Font' appears)

```
┌──────────────────────── Choose Font ──────────────────────────┐
│                                                                │
│  Typefaces:                        Sizes:     Attributes:      │
│  ┌──────────────────────────┐    ┌────┐    ┌───────────────┐   │
│  │ CG Times               ▲ │    │ 6  ▲│    │ [X] Plain      │  │
│  │ CG Triumvirate           │    │ 7  │    │ [ ] Bold       │   │
│  │ Univers Medium      ▶    │    │ 8  │    │ [ ] Italic     │   │
│  │ Futura Bold II           │    │ 9  │    │ [ ] Underline  │   │
│  │ CG Bodoni Bold           │    │ 10 │    │ [ ] Monospace  │   │
│  │ Garamond Antiqua         │    │ 11 │    │ [ ] Small Caps │   │
│  │ Microstyle Bold Extended │    │ 12 │    │ [ ] Subscript  │   │
│  │ Cooper Black           ▼ │    │ 13 │    │ [ ] Superscript│   │
│  └──────────────────────────┘    │ 14 ▼│    └───────────────┘   │
│                                                                │
│                                           < OK >  < Cancel >   │
└────────────────────────────────────────────────────────────────┘
```

You will see that certain options are highlighted. These will probably be CG TIMES, 12, and PLAIN. Thus, the current font is classed as CG Times 12-point Plain. This is the default or standard font but this technique for determining the font can be used any time.

B2. Selecting Text

Having typed in some text, we can now play about with faces, sizes and attributes to see what difference they make. To do this, we need to be able to select blocks or lines of text. We did this earlier but let's do it again.

Move Mouse	(to start of second line of 'The cat...)
Left-Hold	(hold button down)
Move Mouse	(to end of line)
Mouse	(release button)

The second line should now be highlighted and we can change the various elements of the font.

B3. Type Face

First, let's change the type face from a Serif one like CG Times to a Sans Serif one like CG Triumvirate. To do this, leave the second line highlighted and;

Move Mouse	(to Text option on Menu Line)
Left-Click	Text
Left Click	Choose Font
Dialog Box	('Choose Font' appears, see above)
Bottom Line	'Select Font Style, Size and Attributes'
Move Mouse	(over CG Triumvirate)
Left-Click	(to choose this typeface)
Left-Click	< OK >

The box will disappear and the second line of text is now in different face. This font is CG Triumvirate 12 Plain.

B4. Type Sizes

Now, let's change the type size from 12-point to 18 point. To do this, highlight the third line and;

Move Mouse	(to Text option on Menu Line)
Left-Click	Text
Left Click	Choose Font
Dialog Box	('Choose Font' appears, see above)
Bottom Line	'Select Font Style, Size and Attributes'
Move Mouse	(to scroll bar on sizes box, click down-arrow until 18 appears)
Left-Click	(18 to select this size)
Left-Click	< OK >

The box will disappear and the third line of text is now in 18-point. This font is CG Times 18 Plain.

B5. Type Attributes

This time, let's change the type attributes from plain to make it more outstanding. To do this, highlight the fourth line of text and;

Move Mouse	(to Text option on Menu Line)
Left-Click	Text
Left Click	Choose Font
Dialog Box	('Choose Font' appears, see above)
Bottom Line	'Select Font Style, Size and Attributes'
Move Mouse	(Bold option in Attribute section)
Left-Click	(to choose Bold type)
Move Mouse	(Italic option in Attribute section)
Left-Click	(to choose Italic)
Move Mouse	(Underline in Attribute section)
Left-Click	(to choose Underline)
Left-Click	< OK >

The box will disappear and the fourth line of text is now in different face. This font is CG Times 12 Bold, Italic, Underline. This stands out quite a lot.

B6. Changing the Entire Font

Finally, let's change the entire font. To do this, highlight the fifth line and;

Move Mouse	(to Text option on Menu Line)
Left-Click	Text
Left Click	Choose Font
Dialog Box	('Choose Font' appears, see above)
Bottom Line	'Select Font Style, Size and Attributes'
Move Mouse	(over CG Triumvirate)
Left-Click	(to choose this typeface)
Move Mouse	(to scroll bar on sizes box, click down-arrow until 18 appears)
Left-Click	(18 to select this size)
Move Mouse	(Bold option in Attribute section)
Left-Click	(to choose Bold type)
Move Mouse	(Italic option in Attribute section)
Left-Click	(to choose Italic)
Move Mouse	(Underline in Attribute section)
Left-Click	(to choose Underline)
Left-Click	< OK >

The box will disappear and the fifth line of text is now in different face. This font is CG Triumvirate 18 Bold, Italic, Underline. It is quite different from the original default style. You can, of course, select this font combination before entering text. Anything entered will be in the new style you have chosen.

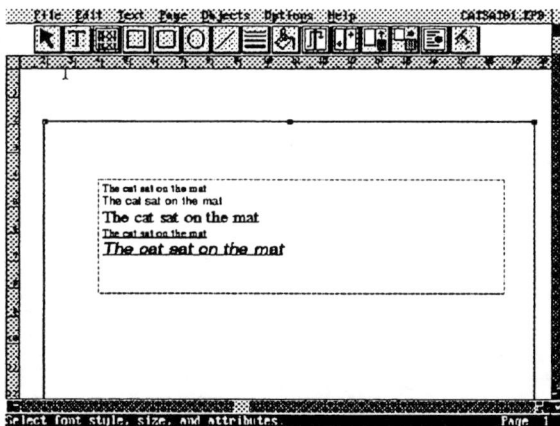

C. Text Formatting

Earlier exercises have shown you all the absolutely essential features of handling text. However, EPDos does contain many more that are contained in the Text Menu on the top line. They mainly concern fine-tuning text in paragraphs. In this section, we will explore their use and how they can give your work professional polish.

It is best we start this section with a clean sheet so to remove the earlier work;

Move Mouse	(to File option on Menu Line)
Left-Click	File
Move Mouse	(to Close option)
Left-Click	Close
Dialog Box	'Warning'

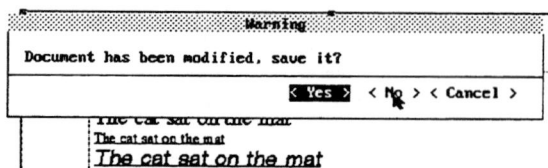

```
                        Warning

  Document has been modified, save it?

                         < Yes >   < No >   < Cancel >
```
```
     The cat sat on the mat
     The cat sat on the mat
     The cat sat on the mat
```

Move Mouse	(to No option)
Left-Click	No

The page will now clear and we can start afresh.

C1. Justifying Text

Justifying text was shown earlier even though it, strictly speaking, falls under the topic of paragraph handling. Read section A7 to remind yourself of exactly how text justification works.

It was detailed earlier on because it is so essential to overall effect a feature whereas the ones below are less important. Their standard or default settings will give perfectly adequate result under most conditions.

C2. Tabulation

Tabulation is for making tables. Primarily. It can also be used for laying out text so that related issues are clearly linked together. For example, you may have a list of major issues with minor ones related to them. The major ones could be flush to the left-hand side of the frame whilst related minor ones start (are indented) 2cm to the right. Even more minor issues could be a further 2cm to the right of this.

Like the other features in this section, tabulation must be applied to at least a whole text frame if not a whole story or document. To see tabulation in action;

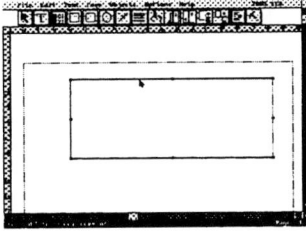

Move Mouse	(to second icon in Toolbox)
Left-Click	
Move Mouse	(to top, left of page)
Left-Hold	(hold down button)
Move Mouse	(down and right for frame 3x13)

You have now created the new text frame. The frame handles should be visible. To apply a tabulation (or other format command) to a frame, these must be obvious to show that the frame has been selected. If they are not, use the Arrow-Head pointer to select the frame first.

Now we must set up the tab points within the frame. There are already a standard set in place every half-inch whereas we want them every 2cms. Moving tabs is a tricky thing to describe so we shall remove all the old ones and then create new ones. So, with the frame selected;

Move Mouse	(to Text option on Menu Line)
Left-Click	Text
Move Mouse	(to Set Tabs option)
Left-Click	Set Tabs
Dialog Box	'Set Tabs' appears
Move Mouse	(onto first triangle depicting tab)
Left-Hold	(hold button down)
Move Mouse	(to the right and off end of tab ruler)
Mouse	(release)

This has now deleted the old tab point. Repeat this for all the other tab points. Now we will create new ones;

Move Mouse	(until Arrow-Head just below 2cm mark on ruler)
Left-Click	(a clear triangle should appear)

Do the same at 4cm and 6cm. These tabs are left-justified, i.e., text will be flush on the left-hand side of the tabs. We can also set up decimal tabs which are very useful when compiling tables based on money values. All the figures will be lined up on the decimal points. This makes a very neat appearance easier to achieve.

To set the decimal tabs;

| Move Mouse | (to 'Decimal tab) |
| Left-Click | Decimal tab |

Move Mouse	(until Arrow-Head just below 8cm
	mark on ruler)
Left-Click	(a black triangle should appear)

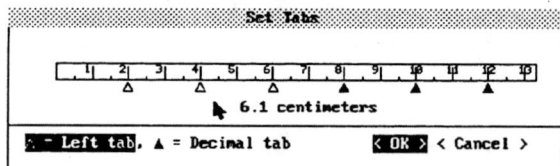

Do this for 10cm and 12cm. Now all the necessary tabs are set and we can return to text entry. First we must decide if we want the tabs applying to just this frame, the story or the whole document.

Move Mouse	(on the < OK > phrase)
Left-Click	< OK >
Dialog Box	'Apply tabs' appears
Move Mouse	(to 'Story' option)
Left-Click	Story
Left-Click	< OK >

You should now be back in the text frame. To demonstrate the formatting possible with tabs, type the following using the Tab key on your keyboard. It may be marked with arrows pointing left and right and touching vertical lines. Remember that the last three figures on the numerical lines are decimal and need decimal points to line up correctly.

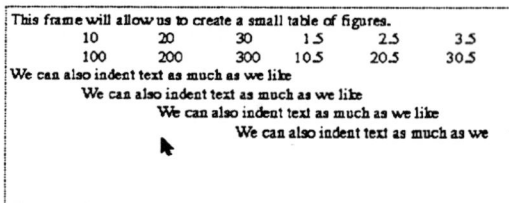

This exercise in tabbing is complete but always keep tabulation in mind. It can help the reader understand things more clearly. Connections can be made more obvious and technical things like statistics communicated more clearly.

C3. Hyphenation

Hyphenation is most important when you have text in fully-justified columns as in a newspaper. Sometimes too many hyphens make sentences harder to follow. Lots of long words can also mean , if hyphenation is not used, that some lines are cramped and others too sparse.

In EPDos, hyphenation is either on or off in a frame, story or document. Using Hyphenation is a simple matter of selecting the frame, Left-Clicking the Text menu, Left-Clicking Hyphenation and then Left-Clicking on 'Enable Hyphenation'.

You are then asked the usual question as to whether to apply hyphenation to just this frame, the story or the whole document.

If you wish to see the problems that can occur, try recreating the text frames below and then substituting lots of long words in the hyphenated frames.

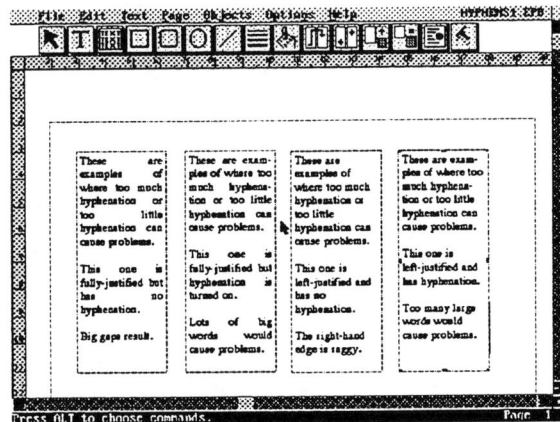

C4. Text Frame Margins

These do two things; they stop the text in a frame clashing with the edges of the frame and they allow you to shape paragraphs with Indents and Outdents.

Remember that the frame edges do not print so the clash is not so important to the reader but it can make life difficult if you choose to edit on-screen. For this reason, a small gap between the text and edge is standard. This is very slight but enough to make a difference. With an oversized frame, you have room to experiment.

115

First we will create four text frames and try out different styles on each. The first two should be around 3cm by 7cm and the last two about half this length. Look at the illustration below to see what to aim for. You want to be able to see all four on-screen at once.

First remove all objects from the current screen by 'closing' the document using the method described at the beginning of this section. Then;

Move Mouse	(to third icon in Toolbox)
Left-Click	
Move Mouse	(to top left of page)
Left-Hold	(hold button down)
Move Mouse	(approx. 3cm to right, 7cm down)
Mouse	(release button)
Type	This is a text frame to test out the effects of various text frame margins. Remember that the on-screen edges of the frame do not print out on paper so the reader will not see them.

When you have done this, do the same for the other three frames and fill them with the same text.

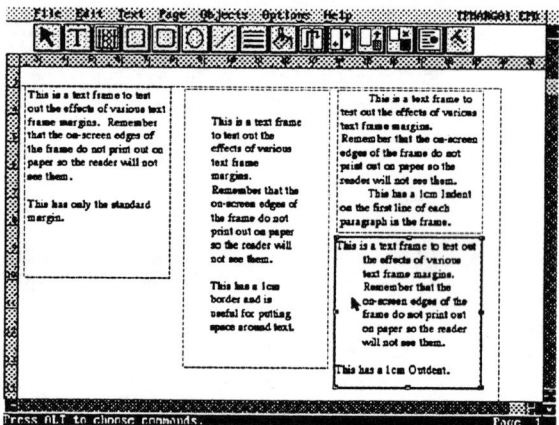

Having created the four frames, we will now give them different margins.

Move Mouse	(to first icon in Toolbox)
Left-Click	Pointer
Move Mouse	(to first text frame)
Left-Click	(to select frame)

Move Mouse	(to Text option on Menu Line)
Left-Click	Text
Move Mouse	(Text Frame Margins option)
Left-Click	Text Frame Margins
Dialog Box	'Text Frame Margins' appears

```
┌──────────────────────────────────────────────┐
│░░░░░░░░░░░░░░░░Text Frame Margins░░░░░░░░░░░░░░┐│
│                                               ││
│  Top: [0.1270] Bottom: [0.1270] (cm)          ││
│                                               ││
│ Left: [0.1270]  Right: [0.1270]               ││
│                                               ││
│   First line indent: [0.0000]                 ││
│                                               ││
│                      < OK >  < Cancel >       ││
└──────────────────────────────────────────────┘
```

This shows the default values for a text frame margin and so we will leave this one alone to judge the others by. Left-Click on < OK >. The Dialog Box 'Apply Formatting' appears so Left-Click < OK >. We now need to select the second text frame and apply a new format to it. Follow the steps at the top of this page again. Then;

Move Mouse	(to 'Top: [0.1270])
Left-Click	(on first zero)
Type	1.000
Move Mouse	(to 'Bottom: [0.1270])
Left-Click	(on first zero)
Type	1.000
Move Mouse	(to 'Left: [0.1270])
Left-Click	(on first zero)
Type	1.000
Move Mouse	(to 'Right: [0.1270])
Left-Click	(on first zero)
Type	1.000
Move Mouse	(to < OK >)
Left-Click	< OK >
Dialog Box	'Apply Formatting' appears
Move Mouse	(to < OK > to accept frame only)
Left-Click	< OK >

You should now see that the entire second frame has been re-composed and that there is a 1cm border all the way around the text. If you ever look at a 'Poetry Corner' in a magazine or paper you will see that this effect is used to make the text stand out from the rather crowded columns used elsewhere.

We now wish to test out the effect of Indents and Outdents. These work in slightly different ways.

Use the methods above to select the third text frame and bring up the 'Text Frame Margins' Dialog Box. To create an Indent, simply change the 'First Line Indent' figure to 1.0000, Left-Click < OK > and then choose to apply it only to the current frame.

You will now see that the first word of the first line has moved 1cm to the right. This is useful in distinguishing paragraphs, especially where narrow columns and tight spacings are used.

To create an Outdent, we must select the frame, bring up the Text Frame Margin Dialog Box and then set the Left margin to 1cm before changing the First Line Indent to -1.000. The reason for this is that the Outdent value cannot be larger than the left margin value, only equal to it smaller than it. Left-Click < OK > and then the 'Apply text Frame Margin' Dialog Box will appear. Apply the Outdent to this frame only and Left-Click < OK >.

The text frame should now have the first line starting 1cm to the left of all the other lines.

> This is a text frame to test out the effects of various text frame margins.
> Remember that the on-screen edges of the frame do not print out on paper so the reader will not see them.
> This has a 1cm Indent on the first line of each paragraph in the frame.

> This is a text frame to test out the effects of various text frame margins. Remember that the on-screen edges of the frame do not print out on paper so the reader will not see them.
> This has a 1cm Outdent.

C5. Character Spacing

EPDos allows you to vary the amount of space between the characters in a frame. This may be done for two main reasons; to make the text fit the allotted space and to create a desired effect. The illustration below shows the effects even small changes can have. Be warned, however, what you see on the screen may not translate quite as well on paper. Print out first to test the effect.

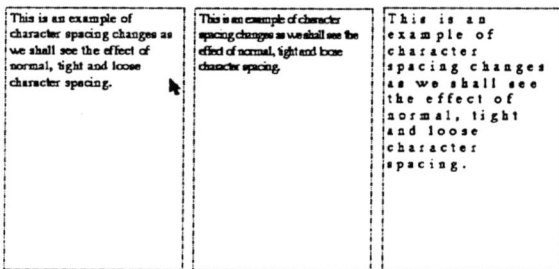

> This is an example of character spacing changes as we shall see the effect of normal, tight and loose character spacing.

> This is an example of character spacing changes as we shall see the effect of normal, tight and loose character spacing.

> This is an example of character spacing changes as we shall see the effect of normal, tight and loose character spacing.

Using the methods detailed above, create three frames the same size, and fill them with the above text. Then select the second frame. We will reduce the spacing by;

Move Mouse	(to Text option on Menu Line)
Left-Click	Text
Move Mouse	(to Character Spacing option)
Left-Click	Character Spacing
Dialog Box	'Character Spacing' appears

Character Spacing

T T T T T T T

< Less > < More > Points: [-1]

< OK > < Cancel >

There are two ways to modify the spacing value which can range from -18 to +36. The first is to repeatedly Left-Click the < Less > or < More > boxes until the desired spacing is achieved. You will see the letter T's change spacing to demonstrate the effect.

However, this tends to under-estimate the effect so best bet is to change the value only a little and then see the effect on-screen. Change it until it is reading -2 the left-click < OK >. You will then see the 'Apply Formatting' Dialog Box as usual so only apply the new value to the current frame selected.

The second method can be demonstrated if we increase the spacing in the third frame. Select this frame and the Character Spacing option from the Text menu. Then, in the Dialog Box, place the pointer over the number, Left-Click it and then type a new value of 5. Again, it is hard to estimate the effect the new value will have. Left-Click < OK > and apply the format only to the frame.

Tight spacing allows more text in a column and loosely-spaced text looks very modern. However, it is easy to overdo both the extent that they become unreadable.

One bizarre effect can be make text read backwards if you make the spacing too tight. This has creative possibilities. E.g., backwards becomes 'sdrawkcab'. Try this with a large frame and a value of -18 !

C6. Kerning

In the example above, we saw how we could make all letters move closer together or further apart. However, for certain combinations of letters, exceptions have to be made so that their spacing is modified further. The classic example is 'WA. '.

W A   Normal Spacing

WA   Kerned Spacing

119

Without Kerning, it is common for the normal gap to be mis-interpreted as the gap between two words. This can make comprehension more difficult. Unfortunately, it is extremely difficult to demonstrate this effect in EPDos.

There are two reasons. The screen resolution is low and at normal type sizes the effect is hardly noticeable. Thus, Kerning is applied to the whole document or not at all and only on type sizes of a certain size and above. It also slows down screen text refreshing and so it is best applied only to headlines and banners where a lack would be obvious.

To change the Kerning Value.

Move Mouse	(to Text option on Menu line)
Left-Click	Text
Move Mouse	(to Kerning option)
Left-click	Kerning
Dialog Box	'Kerning' will appear
Move Mouse	(to [ ] Kerning box)
Left-Click	Kerning
Move Mouse	(to [12] points)
Left-Click	12
Type	14
Left-Click	< OK >

C7. Line Spacing

EPDos allows you to vary the amount of space between the lines in a frame. This may be done for two main reasons; to make the text fit the allotted space and to create a desired effect. The illustration below shows the effects even small changes can have. Be warned, however, what you see on the screen may not translate quite as well on paper. Print out first to test the effect.

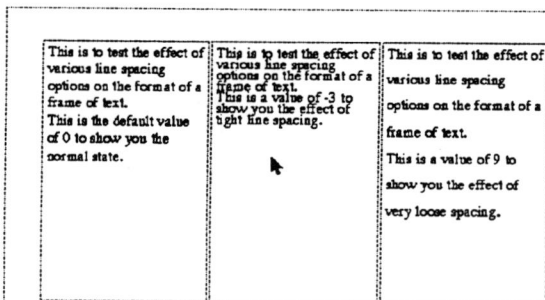

| This is to test the effect of various line spacing options on the format of a frame of text. This is the default value of 0 to show you the normal state. | This is to test the effect of various line spacing options on the format of a frame of text. This is a value of -3 to show you the effect of tight line spacing. | This is to test the effect of various line spacing options on the format of a frame of text. This is a value of 9 to show you the effect of very loose spacing. |

Using the methods detailed above, create three frames the same size, and fill them with the above text. Then select the second frame. We will reduce the spacing by;

Move Mouse	(to Text option on Menu Line)
Left-Click	Text
Move Mouse	(to Line Spacing option)
Left-Click	Line Spacing
Dialog Box	'Line Spacing' appears

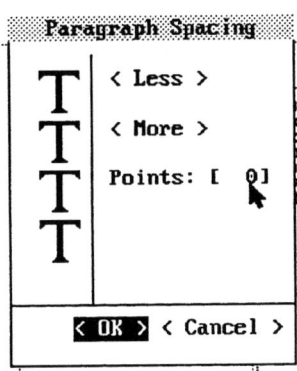

Paragraph Spacing

< Less >

< More >

Points: [0]

< OK > < Cancel >

There are two ways to modify the spacing value which can range from -18 to +72. The first is to repeatedly Left-Click the < Less > or < More > boxes until the desired spacing is achieved. You will see the letter T's change spacing to demonstrate the effect.

However, this tends to under-estimate the effect so best bet is to change the value only a little and then see the effect on-screen. Change it until it is reading -3 the left-click < OK >. You will then see the 'Apply Formatting' Dialog Box as usual so only apply the new value to the current frame selected.

The second method can be demonstrated if we increase the spacing in the third frame. Select this frame and the Line Spacing option from the Text menu. Then, in the Dialog Box, place the pointer over the number, Left-Click it and then type a new value of +9. Again, it is hard to estimate the effect the new value will have. Left-Click < OK > and apply the format only to the frame.

C8. Paragraph Spacing

EPDos allows you to vary the amount of space between the paragraphs in a frame. This may be done for two main reasons; to make the text fit the allotted space and to create a desired effect. The illustration below shows the effects even small changes can have. Be warned, however, what you see on the screen may not translate quite as well on paper. Print out first to test the effect.

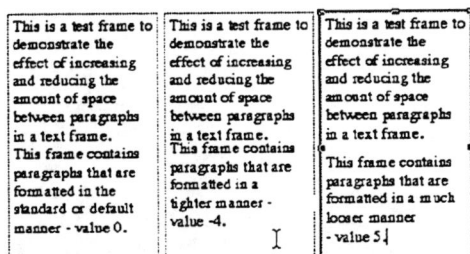

This is a test frame to demonstrate the effect of increasing and reducing the amount of space between paragraphs in a text frame. This frame contains paragraphs that are formatted in the standard or default manner - value 0.	This is a test frame to demonstrate the effect of increasing and reducing the amount of space between paragraphs in a text frame. This frame contains paragraphs that are formatted in a tighter manner - value -4.	This is a test frame to demonstrate the effect of increasing and reducing the amount of space between paragraphs in a text frame. This frame contains paragraphs that are formatted in a much looser manner - value 5.

121

Using the methods detailed above, create three frames the same size, and fill them with the above text. Then select the second frame. We will reduce the spacing by;

Move Mouse	(to Text option on Menu Line)
Left-Click	Text
Move Mouse	(to Paragraph Spacing option)
Left-Click	Paragraph Spacing
Dialog Box	'Paragraph Spacing' appears

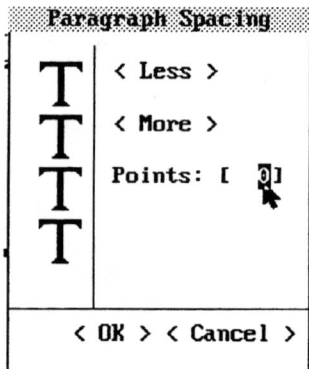

Paragraph Spacing

T
T
T
T
T

< Less >

< More >

Points: [0]

< OK > < Cancel >

There are two ways to modify the spacing value which can range from -18 to +72. The first is to repeatedly Left-Click the <Less> or < More > boxes until the desired spacing is achieved. You will see the letter T's change spacing to demonstrate the effect.

However, this tends to under-estimate the effect so best bet is to change the value only a little and then see the effect on-screen. Change it until it is reading -2 the left-click < OK >. You will then see the 'Apply Formatting' Dialog Box as usual so only apply the new value to the current frame selected.

The second method can be demonstrated if we increase the spacing in the third frame. Select this frame and the Paragraph Spacing option from the Text menu. Then, in the Dialog Box, place the pointer over the number, Left-Click it and then type a new value of 5. Again, it is hard to estimate the effect the new value will have. Left-Click < OK > and apply the format only to the frame.

C9. Paragraph Text Styles

You have now seen and used all the formatting commands that EPDos has to offer. However, there are so many combinations of these that it could be very tedious applying these repeatedly across a large publication. There is also the possibility of making a mistake that is not obvious until printing time.

For this reason, the formatting combinations can be kept as 'Styles' that can be applied to individual paragraphs. In many ways, this is much more flexible than the normal method of applying individual formats to frame, stories or documents.

With Styles, you can apply several different formats in one frame of text. For example, headlines and main text can be held in one large frame not two separate ones.

To create a new style you must create a text frame and add text to it. Then format this text using the normal commands until you are happy with it. Highlight it, then;

Move Mouse	(to Text option on Menu Line)
Left-Click	Text
Move Mouse	(to Create Style)
Left-Click	Create Style
Dialog Box	'Create a Style' appears

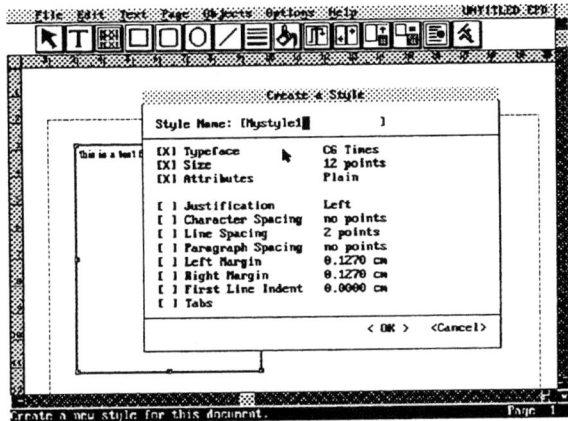

As you can see, all the options you've set individually are now shown together with a space for you to give a name to this new style. You may find that certain options are not set correctly. These will probably have 'Xs' in the boxes to the left. Click on these to remove the X and the right option should appear.

| Left-Click | (the Style Name box) |
| Type | Mystyle1 |

Try this exercises with various combinations of attributes. Choose a type face and size you like and format paragraphs in the way you prefer. Experiment !

Now it is time to apply your new style. Using the Text Frame tool, create a large-ish text frame on the page. Now enter a passage of text from a favourite book or copy something from a magazine.

Choosing which text to apply a particular style to can be in done in several ways depending on how much you want doing. You can select paragraph by paragraph simply by placing Left-Clicking the Text tool and then placed the I-Beam pointer in the relevant paragraph, left-Clicking and then choosing the correct style.

123

Alternatively, you can re-style several paragraphs at once by placing the I-Beam pointer at the start of the first and then holding the button down and moving to the last paragraph in order to highlight the required ones. You then choose the style as below.

You may also want to apply a new style to the whole of a story. This is done by the following method;

Move Mouse	(to one of frames in story)
Left-Click	(to select frame)
Move Mouse	(to Edit option on Menu Line)
Left-Click	Edit
Move Mouse	(down to Select Entire Story option)
Left-Click	Select Entire Story

Every piece of text in the story in every linked frame should now be highlighted ready for a style to be applied.

To apply a pre-defined style;

Move Mouse	(to Text option on Menu Line)
Left-Click	Text
Move Mouse	(to Choose Style option)
Left-Click	Choose Style
Dialog Box	'Choose Style' appears

Move Mouse	(to scroll bars, down arrow)
Left-Click	(until you can see 'Mystyle1')
Left-Click	Mystyle1

Move Mouse	(to < OK >)
Left-Click	< OK >

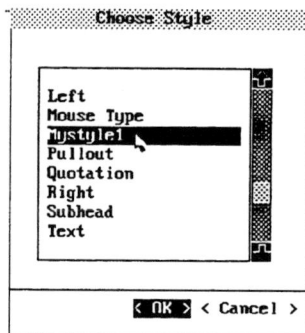

You should now see that 'Mystyle1' has been applied to all the paragraphs you highlighted. Your new style would be saved along with any documents you put onto disk.

You can also save a style as part of any template you create for future use.

Occasionally, you may wish to delete some of the styles present. This makes sense when you have made up your own and do not want the pre-defined ones. Sometimes you will find that scrolling through all the unwanted ones takes too much time.

To delete a style (e.g., 'Bulleted 3');

Move Mouse	(to Text option on Menu Line)
Left-Click	Text
Move Mouse	(to Delete Style option)
Left-Click	Delete Style
Dialog Box	'Delete Style' appears
Move Mouse	(to scroll bars)
Left-Click	(until 'Bulleted 3' seen)
Left-Click	Bulleted 3
Move Mouse	(to < OK >)
Left-Click	< OK >
Dialog Box	'Warning' will appear

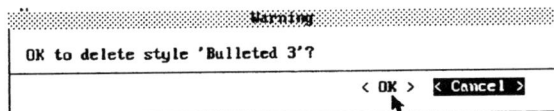

```
:::::::::::::::::::::::::::::::::::::::::Warning::::::::::::::::::::::::::::::::::::::::::
OK to delete style 'Bulleted 3'?
                                              < OK >  < Cancel >
                                                  ▲
```

Left-Click	< OK >

You can repeat this process for all styles you wish to delete in future.

Chapter 8.   Handling Graphics

A. The Basics
   A1. The Shape Toolbox   128
   A2. Boxes and Rounded Boxes   128
   A3. Circles and Ellipses   129
   A4. Fills and Objects   130
   A5. Drawing and Setting Lines   131

B. Manipulating Graphics
   B1. Graphics and the Grid   132
   B2. Selecting and Moving   134
   B3. Resizing and Shaping   134
   B4. Stacking and Layering   135
   B5. Aligning and Equating   137
   B6. Cutting and Pasting   138
   B7. Copying and Duplicating   140
   B8. Specifications   142

C. Importing Pictures and Graphics
   C1. Issues Involved   144
   C2. Suitable Formats   144
   C3. Clip Art   144
   C4. Importing a Picture   145
   C5. Editing Pictures   145
   C6. Rotating and Flipping   145
   C7. Transparent and Solid Pictures 147
   C8. Crop Image   147
   C9. Reversing Colours   148
   C10.Edit Bit Image   148
   C11.Saving as a Picture   149

A. The Basics

A1. The Shape Toolbox

These six icons in the Toolbox form the basis of grpahics creation in EPDos. However, it must be stressed that EPDos is not a fully-fledged graphics package. It will not produce freehand or skilled artwork.

However, even the most basic tools such as these can be used to produce effective results with a little time and patience This book will tell you how to use the tools but it is up your imagination to combine them effectively.

A2. Boxes and Rounded Boxes

Apart from their use in creating graphics, the Box and Rounded Box tools are excellent for giving a 'look' to your publication. This can be done by putting borders around blocks of text and photos to separate them from each other or indicate they are linked.

For example, in the main part of an article, you may use a term that you don't think many of your readers will understand. What you can do is use a box to put another text frame in that includes an explanation. Shading this box (see Fills later on) can make the explanation stand out even further.

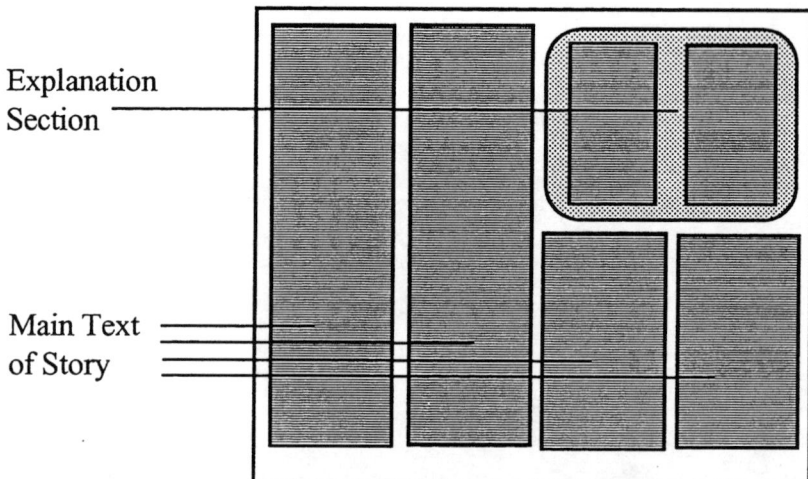

Explanation
Section

Main Text
of Story

To use either of these shapes;

Move Mouse   (to Box/Rounded Box in Toolbox)

Left-Click   or

Move Mouse   (onto page)
Left-Hold   (hold button down)
Move Mouse   (to the left and down)
Mouse   (release button)

You will now see the Box or Rounded Box on your page. The thickness of the line can also be altered (see Lines).

To create a genuinely square box;

CTRL   (hold CTRL key down)
Mouse Move   (to Box you want to square
Left-Click
CTRL   (release CTRL key)

The Square will take the shortest diameter of the Box as its size. To get the right size may mean several attempts.

A3.   Circles and Ellipses

Not everything in this world is square but many publications can seem so. Therefore, it can be a pleasant change to see something circular or elliptical (a squashed circle). To create an Ellipse;

Move Mouse   (to Ellipse icon in Toolbox)

Left-Click

Move Mouse   (onto page)
Left-Hold   (hold button down)
Move Mouse   (to the left and down)
Mouse   (release button)

To create a Circle;

CTRL   (hold CTRL key down)
Mouse Move   (to ellipse you want circular)
Left-Click
CTRL   (release CTRL key)

The circle will take the shortest diameter of the ellipse as its size. To get the right size may mean several attempts.

129

A4. Fills and Objects

Having drawn an object you may want to fill it in for effect, i.e., shade it or give it a pattern. EPDos has quite a number of features in this respect. To test it out, draw a Box, Square Box, Ellipse and Circle on the same page.

To fill the rectangle;

Move Mouse	(over rectangle)
Left-Click	(to select rectangle)
Move Mouse	(to Set Fill icon in Toolbox)
Left-Click	

Dialog Box   'Set Fill' appears

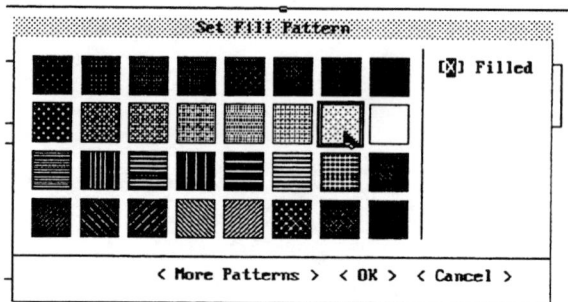

Move Mouse	(to a lightly shaded box on the second row, 7th from left)
Left-Click	(to use this fill)
Move Mouse	(to < OK >)
Left-Click	< OK >

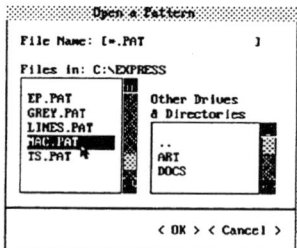

The frame you highlighted should now be lightly shaded. However, EPDos has many more patterns up its sleeve. The set you have just seen on screen are kept in a file called 'EP.PAT'. There are others called 'GRAY.PAT', 'LINES.PAT', 'MAC.PAT', and 'TS.PAT'. You can call these up by Left-Clicking < More Patterns > when it appears in the 'Set Fill Pattern, Dialog Box (see above). Then Left-Click twice rapidly to load the file.

Some of these patterns are much more interesting than the standard ones, especially the 'MAC.PAT' ones. They are well worth exploring when you have a little time.

Try filling the other shapes with different textures using the method outlined above and the 'More Patterns' option.

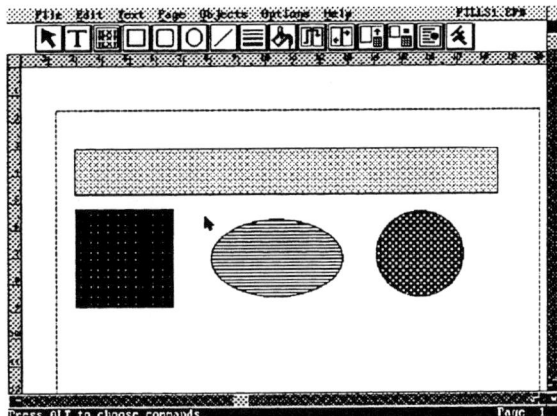

These are just a few of the many patterns available. Fills can also be used to create effects such as shadows and reliefs and some patterns, such as the brickwork one, help when trying to draw buildings etc.

A5. Drawing and Setting Lines

Lines can serve any number of purposes in a document. They can be used as part of an illustration, to separate pieces of text, to indicate layout, to underline etc., etc.

Before drawing any line (or Box, Ellipse etc.) it is a good idea to specify what type of line you would like drawing. You have a choice of thicknesses, whether the lines are black or white or do not print out on paper (they are only ever seen on the screen).

To set the line thickness;

Left-Click

Dialog Box	'Set Line Type' appears
Move Mouse	(to second line down)
Left-click	(second line down)
Move Mouse	(to 'Black' option)
Left-Click	Black
Left-Click	< OK >

Set Line Type

Thickness	Ink
	( ) Black
	( ) White
	( ) Non-Printing

< OK >   <Cancel>

This has now set the line thickness and colour. To draw a straight line in any direction;

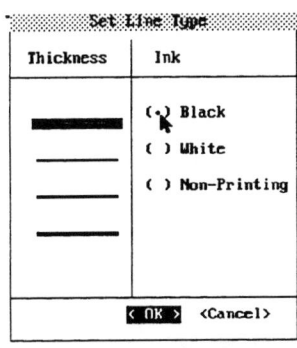

131

| Move Mouse | (to Line icon in Toolbox) |
| Left-Click | |

Move Mouse	(onto page)
Left-Hold	(hold button down)
Move Mouse	(around to see length and direction change until you are happy with it)
Mouse	(release button)

You will now see a line in the direction you set. However, you will often want a line that is accurately vertical or horizontal. To create a Vertical or Horizontal Line;

CTRL	(hold CTRL key down)
Mouse Move	(to line you want to alter)
Left-Click	
CTRL	(release CTRL key)

The line will become horizontal or vertical depending upon which has the smaller angle to travel.

B.   *Manipulating Graphics*

B1.   *Graphics and the Grid*

A blank sheet of paper can be a bit daunting for someone who isn't used to laying out pages. One very useful feature in EPDos is the Grid. This is not printed but can be shown on the screen and helps you to position text and pictures. It also allows you to maintain constant gaps between items such as columns.

To set the Grid;

Move Mouse	(to Options option on Menu Line)
Left-Click	Options
Move Mouse	(to Set Grids option)
Left-Click	Set Grids
Dialog Box	'Set Grid Size' appears

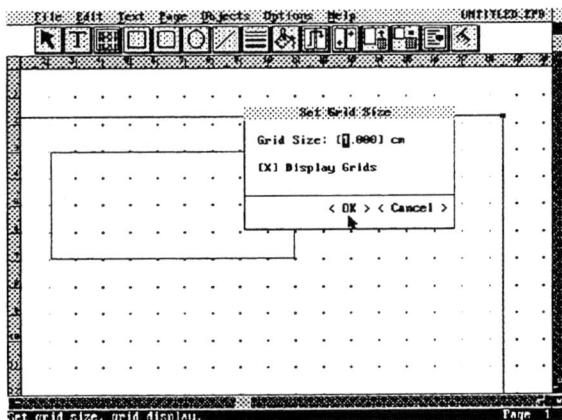

Move Mouse	(over the grid size figure)
Left-Click	(to highlight number)
Type	1.000
Move Mouse	(to 'Display Grid' box)
Left-Click	(to turn grid display on)
Left-Click	< OK >

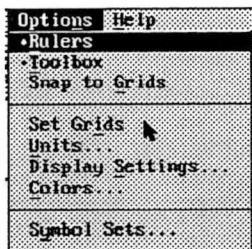

You will now see little dots all across and down the page and beyond it. Too many dots can cause problems as they can confuse the page objects but too few are of little use. The best way to use the grid is only when you need to. When you have altered your layout and are happy with, turn the grid off. If you want help lining objects up with the grid, Left-Click the 'Snap to Grids' option in the Options menu. This will do it automatically for you.

133

B2. Selecting and Moving

In the chapter on text handling, you were shown how to move a text frame. Simply move the mouse to the edge of the object and Left-Hold and move the mouse to the new position. However, you may want to move certain elements together so that they stay in relative position to each other. If you've painstakingly drawn a house with the Toolbox and realise it should be on the other side, you wouldn't want to move each piece in turn.

Fortunately in EPDos, you can 'Group' items, including text so that if you move one, you move them all by the same amount and in the same direction.

With the Box and Ellipse tools, draw a wide rectangle with a circle through it (see below). Then;

Hold-Shift	(hold the SHIFT key down)
Move Mouse	(to inside of the rectangle)
Left-Click	(to select rectangle - handles appear)
Move Mouse	(to inside of circle)
Left-Click	(to select circle - handles appear)
Left-Hold	(to group two objects together)
Move Mouse	(to new position)

You will see that box items have moved in unison as in the illustration below;

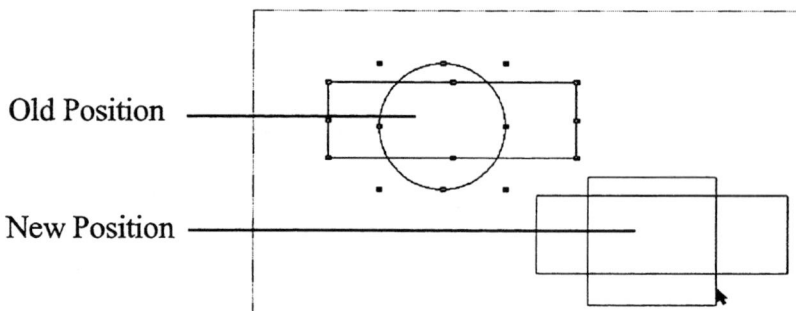

Old Position

New Position

B3. Resizing and Shaping

When you resize an object you retain its original shape or proportions. For example, if an object is 5cm by 10cm then its proportions are 1:2. If you change its size to 10cm by 20cm or 2.5cm by 5cm, you have changed size and not proportion or shape. It is still 1:2. If you reshape, however, these proportions are lost. A wide object may become thinner or taller etc.

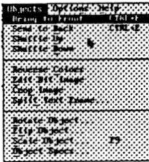

To resize an object, you must use the Scale Object option from the Objects menu. First draw a small rectangle, then do the following;

Move Mouse	(to edge of rectangle)
Left-Click	(to select rectangle)
Move Mouse	(to Objects option in Menu Line)
Left-Click	Objects
Move Mouse	(to Scale Objects option)
Left-Click	Scale Objects
Dialog Box	'Scale Object' appears

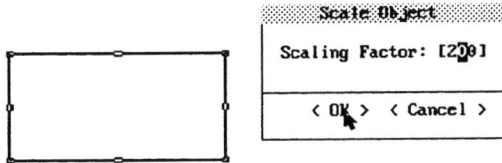

Change the 100 in the Scaling factor box to 200 and then Left-Click < OK >. The small rectangle is now a lot larger but the shape is the same. Note that the 200 doubles the length of each side. This effectively multiplies the area by four times not twice.

If you wanted to double the area, you must find out the square root of the multiple, i.e., the root of 2.00 which is approx. 1.4 and multiply by 100 (the result is 140 roughly). To treble the area, find the root of 3.00 and multiply by 100. Try a few out.

To reshape an object, Left-Click one of its edges. Then Left-Hold a handle and move the mouse (drag the handle). Corner handles move horizontally and vertically. Middle-of-line ones move one-dimensionally.

B4. Stacking and Layering

When you have a number of objects (text, pictures, shapes) some will probably overlap or completely cover others. This is use to create effects such as the example in Section A2 where the explanation box used text overlaid on a filled box to make it stand out. The filled box was at the 'back' and the text at the 'front'.

However, you can have many layers and this is where layer control comes in. You can 'shuffle' an object up and down to put it where you want in the pile of layers. In the example mentioned, you could have a white square behind the text to emphasise it even more.

One very useful effect is 'Shadowing'. To do this, you place a filled object of the same size and shape behind another and then offset the filled object slightly. The example below shows you how. First, draw square Box 5cm by 5cm and fill it paper-white. Then;

Move Mouse	(to Edit option on Menu Line)
Left-Click	Edit
Move Mouse	(to Duplicate option)
Left-Click	Duplicate

A second 5x5 square will appear. Move the mouse to the Set Fill Icon and Left-Click. Choose a lightly-shaded fill and then Left-Click < OK >. The top box (at the front) will be fully visible and the paper-white one mainly hidden by it. To reverse this;

Move Mouse	(to Objects option on Menu Line)
Left-Click	Objects
Move Mouse	(to Shuffle Down option)
Move Mouse	(off the page)
Left-Click	(to remove box selection handles)

Now you will see the shadow effect. It is even better if you select the filled box and use the Set Lines icon to remove the box edge. This is more authentic as a shadow's soft edge.

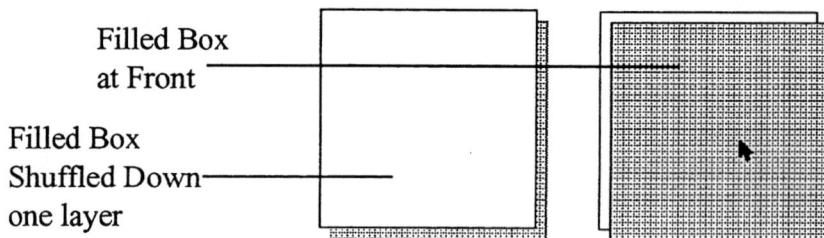

Filled Box at Front

Filled Box Shuffled Down one layer

The example above only gives you a slight taste of the power and effect that layering can have on graphics, text and pictures. For example, if drawing a house, the chimney can be made to appear either on the front roof or on the back roof simply by changing the layering.

The best way to learn about layering is simply to practice and experiment. Use the effect to create a feeling of 'depth' or perspective in your graphics and text.

136

B5. *Aligning and Equating*

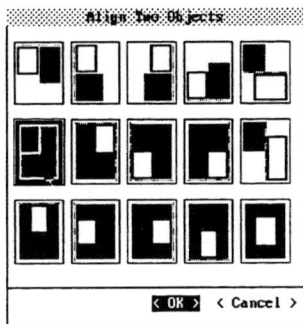

EPDos has a number of facilities aimed to make designing graphics easier. Two important ones are Aligning and Equating. Aligning ensures that two objects are lined up in a particular way or format.

There are many formats to choose from. For example, you may want the top edges of two Boxes to be level. Maybe you want them side-by-side, one inside the other etc., etc. You can see the variety from the 'Align Two Objects' Dialog Box to the left.

The shaded box represent the first object you select, the 'primary', and the white box is the 'secondary'. The secondary object is always moved to the primary object. To see this in action, first drawn two circles of differing sizes and a few cm apart. For this exercise, we shall always use the larger one as the primary (it does not have to be normally. Then;

Move Mouse	(to the 12th icon in the Toolbox)
Left-Click	
Bottom Line	'Select a primary and secondary object' appears
Pointer	(changes to a crooked, double-headed arrow shape)
Move Mouse	(into the larger circle, the primary)
Left-Click	(to select primary object)
Move Mouse	(to smaller circle, the secondary)
Left-Click	(to select secondary object)
Dialog Box	'Align Two Objects' appears

You now have fifteen options to choose from. The best way to learn of what effect they have is just to keep trying different ones. For this exercise, though, we shall use the one in the top left-hand corner.

Move Mouse	(to icon in top left corner)
Left-Click	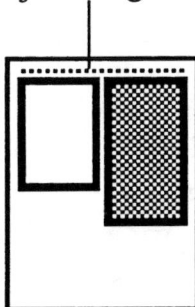
Left-Click	< OK >

Dotted Line that Objects Align to

The objects are both now aligned to the top edge of the larger, primary circle. In the blow-up, you can see the Dotted Line in the icon that indicates how the objects will be lined up. This is very faint but provides a useful guide.

137

Equating objects is very straight forward. This will turn two different objects into the same size. Again, start with two circles of differing sizes. Then;

Move Mouse	(to 13th icon in Toolbox)
Left-Click	
Bottom Line	'Select a primary and secondary object' appears
Pointer	(changes to an '=' sign)
Move Mouse	(to primary object)
Left-Click	(to select primary object)
Move Mouse	(to secondary object)
Left-Click	(to select secondary object)

The two circles should now be the same size as the primary circle.

B6. Cutting and Pasting

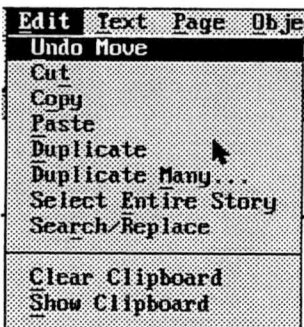

Nobody gets everything right first time. Therefore, you need the facility to remove and move objects, be they text, drawings or pictures. This is no different to the old-fashioned hand method of 'Cutting and Pasting' used in the publishing industry for aeons.

In newspapers, a story was created as one long column of text that was then cut to size and pasted into to fit the page layout. If the layout changed, e.g., a hot news story came in at the last moment, the columns could be re-cut and re-pasted elsewhere. Only at the last second, when the plates, films or whatever were made up, could no further manipulation be done.

Computerised systems have what is known as a 'Clipboard' where pieces of text or objects can be stored temporarily. This is especially valuable when moving text from one page to another.

IMPORTANT NOTE 1: When you cut or copy any object to the Clipboard, it remains there only so long as you do not cut or copy anything else. Current contents are always replaced by newer ones.

IMPORTANT NOTE 2: You can view what is currently in the Clipboard. However, the shape may seem distorted. Ignore this, when you re-paste the object it will be restored to its original size and shape.

138

To do an exercise in cutting and pasting, you should create four tall rectangular boxes and place a small circle in one of them as shown below.

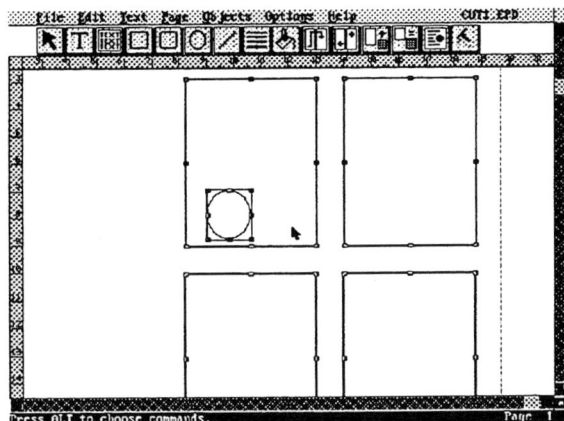

You must now select them all, starting with the circle and keeping you finger on the shift key to 'group' them together for cutting and pasting. When all are selected;

Move Mouse	(to Edit option on Menu Line)
Left-Click	Edit
Move Mouse	(to Cut option)
Left-Click	Cut

The entire graphic should now disappear from your screen. Do not be alarmed. Let's look at it in the Clipboard using the 'Show Clipboard' option.

Move Mouse	(to Edit option on Menu Line)
Left-Click	Edit
Move Mouse	(to Show Clipboard option)
Left-Click	Show Clipboard

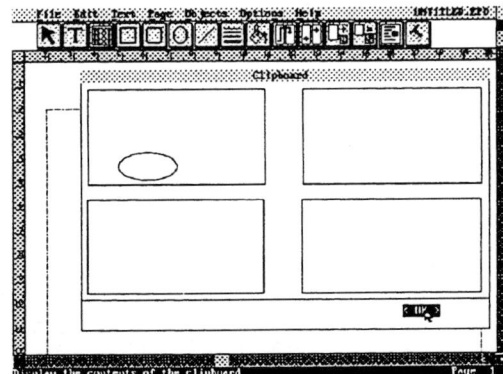

139

As you can see, the shape has been distorted. Left-Click < OK > to return to the blank page. To restore the image;

Move Mouse	(to Edit option on Menu Line)
Left-Click	Edit
Move Mouse	(to Paste option)
Left-Click	Paste

The five objects should now reappear in the same place as before and in the same proportions. Of course, you do not have to re-paste the objects. You could just leave them cut if you want to remove them permanently.

Also, you would not normally paste them back into the same position. As you can move groups of objects together on one page without using cutting and pasting (by the dragging method shown earlier), you would normally use cutting and pasting only to move to another page (or even document if you load a new one).

You should also note that the Clipboard still contains the five objects. Therefore, you can paste the same objects into different positions in a document. For example, a logo may be used at the top of each page.

B7. Copying and Duplicating

You can also copy objects to the Clipboard. The fundamental difference between this and cutting is that the original image is left in place. When repeating objects on different pages, this is safer than cutting as you do not risk losing the original.

Copy can also be used to cut and paste more safely. To do this, copy the object, paste it into the various new positions and then, when you are satisfied, cut the original. You still have other copies for later use.

Duplicating is a quicker form of copy and pasting as it is done in one step only. There are two forms of Duplicate. The first one create a copy that it places just slightly away from the original. This is handy for shadow effects and overlapping copies etc. You can then position the dupe.

Duplicate Many will create a pattern of copies around the screen in a set order and arrangement. this form of duplicate can be used to create many artisitic effects that would be laborius to do by hand. The dupes can be off-set and either enlarge or shrink in series. See diagram.

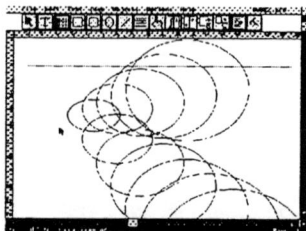

140

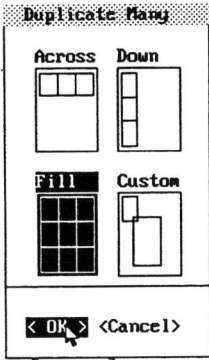

To duplicate and object many times, first draw a small ellipse in the top left corner. Then;

Move Mouse	(to Edit option on Menu Line)
Left-Click	Edit
Move Mouse	(to Duplicate Many option)
Left-Click	Duplicate Many
Dialog Box	'Duplicate Many' appears

There are four patterns to choose from; to copy across only, down only, fill (across and down), or to create a custom pattern. The first three will make the specified number of exact dupes and space them apart by a set amount. This amount can vary. Positive numbers will offset the new dupes leaving a gap. Negative numbers will cause overlapping objects to appear. Both are useful.

Left-Click	(bottom left Icon - Fill)
Left-Click	< OK >
Dialog Box	'Duplicate Many' will appear

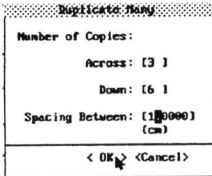

Set the number across to 3 and down to 6 with spacing between of 1.0000 cm and then click < OK >. This will create the pattern shown below.

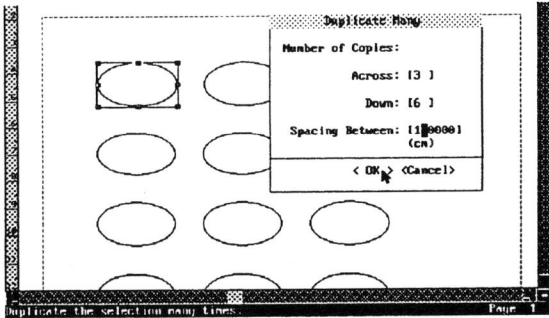

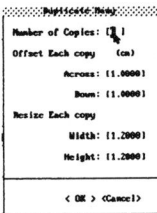

The Custom option is more complex but allows more creative scope as you can see below. This is the result of the same ellipse being duped, off-set and enlarge in two directions by applying 'Duplicate Many' twice.

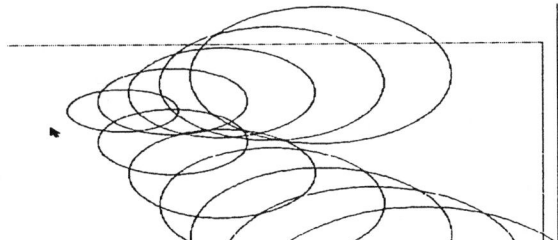

Again, the best way to learn about Duplicate Many is simply to 'play' with objects and to try and create certain effects such as circles-in-circles, wall-paper (offset to the right and half the object height downwards) and thought-bubbles (as used in comics and advertising).

B8. Specifications

The low-resolution screens supported by EPDos mean that it is often very difficult to gauge precisely how large an object is. In some work this may be crucially important and for this reason you can find out the object's specification using the 'Object Spec' option.

Not only will this allow you to inspect the size etc., it will also allow you to specify the ones that you want.

Draw a Rectangle, then;

Move Mouse	(to Objects option on Menu Line)
Left-Click	Objects
Move Mouse	(to Object Spec option)
Left-Click	Object Spec
Dialog Box	'Object Specifications' appears

```
░░░░░░░░░░░░░░░Object Specifications░░░░░░░░░░░░░░░

Placement on Page                      [X] Printable
  From Top:    [3.0300] cm              [X] Selectable
  From Left:   [2.3200]                 [ ] Hidden
                                        [ ] Locked
Dimensions                              [ ] Filled
  Width:       [4.1600]                 [ ] Wrap Around
  Height:      [5.3700]

Name:          [RECTANGLE       ]    │ 48 bytes

                                    < OK >   <Cancel>
```

You will see the objects details covering size, place on page, type, storage space and other features. You can change any you want and the effects will occur when you Left-Click < OK >. The other effects are;

Printable
This determines whether an object is seen on the screen and printed out or only seen on the screen. This can be useful when using objects to help layout or leaving comments to aid later use such as 'place chart here'.

Selectable
With this option chosen, you cannot select the object until you change this option again. With large or complex graphics, it is easy to select and alter the wrong object.

Hidden

You may sometimes want to hide an object occassionally. For example, you might want to see if a photo looks better with or without a border.

Locked

If you lock an object, it cannot be moved or re-sized. You can still do other things such as fill or enter text. The text frames loaded with a template are locked in place to stop accidental movement etc.

Filled

With this option, objects are either filled (i.e. cannot be seen through) or are unfilled (i.e. transparent, can be seen through to other objects).

Wrap Around

A fuller explanation is contained later in this book. However, in brief, text can be forced to flow around (rather than over or under) a graphic or picture. See the illustration to the side for a better idea.

djjjfgj jhjhjjhjj djhfnhj
fdjhgf j ddkjfd]
iueiue iurfiuriu
friufiuyu hrifrior
ejgg riorior rioreiorr

Auto Import

This is used in conjunction with the Template commands. Basically, you can use this to automate the production of a document which is useful if others word on it to.

When you define a frame and change its spec to include the Auto Import feature it means that when the template is loaded, you will be asked for the name of a word-processing file which contains the text of the story. If the story flows over more than one linked frame then this will be done automatically.

The basic idea is that each story is compiled beforehand using a word-processor which is undoubtedly better and faster than the average DTP package for this purpose. It also means that several people can work on their own machines and then the final 'paste-up' done centrally.

C. Importing Pictures and Graphics

C1. What Can Be Imported ?

EPDos allows graphics and pictures to be 'imported' or incorporated into documents from many packages and in many popular formats.

These can either have originated in a computer package designed for this purpose or it can have been scanned into the computer from photos, hand-drawn artwork, direct from cameras (e.g. videos), etc.

EPDos does not directly support these programs so you must make sure that their output is in a file format that EPDos is capable of reading and re-creating.

C2. Suitable Formats

PCX, TIFF,
CGM, MAC,
ART, NAM,
IMG, GIF,
EPS

EPDos can use any of the formats listed to the left. These cover nearly all the major formats and most other packages can output files in many different ones so it is simply a matter of choosing a suitable one. The most popular ones are TIFF, PCX and CGM which you will find in virtually every program handling images.

If you can, it is best to put colour pictures into black-and-white or grey-scale files as EPDos 2 does not support colour and some colour images will translate very badly. To get it right in the graphics package is better.

C3. Clip Art

This is extremely useful. Clip art is designed to help non-artists incorporate generic graphics into documents. Say you wanted a drawing of an airliner in an article but are not worried about make, type, etc., you could buy a file of pre-drawn clip art and choose the one you liked. There is a huge amount available.

It is unlikely you fill find exactly the one you want but there are usually enough in the right vein that you can choose one suitable. For a regular column on travel, it doesn't matter what type of plane is used. An old monoplane would do to get the message across.

EPDos comes with a small number of clip-art images but more can be purchased. If you decide to purchase a separate graphics package, check to see how many images are included. One package has 14,500 !

C4. Importing a Picture

Importing or loading a picture into EPDos is relatiely straightforward. The Clip Art included is held in a directory called 'C:\EXPRESS\ART' and you can also use this directory to keep other artwork.

Move Mouse	(to File option on Menu Line)
Left-Click	File
Move Mouse	(to Import a Picture option)
Left-Click	Import a Picture
Dialog Box	'Import a Picture' appears

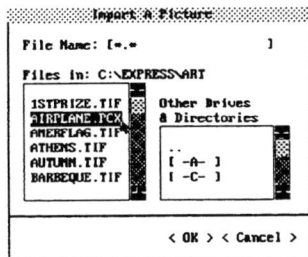

You can move the mouse to the File Name : [ ] box and type the name in or you can use the scroll bars to find the one you want and then Double-Click it or left-Click to highlight it and then Left-Click < OK >. You could also load pictures from floppy disks by changing the drive if you Left-Click [A].

Your desired picture should now be on the page.

C5. Editing Pictures

You can treat pictures just like the other objects. You can cut, paste, copy, duplicate, re-size, re-shape, find out the specification etc., etc. However, you can also do one or two things extra.

C6. Rotating and Flipping

Pictures can be Rotated or Flipped. The former is similar turning the picture around in a circle whereas the latter is like reflecting it in a mirror.

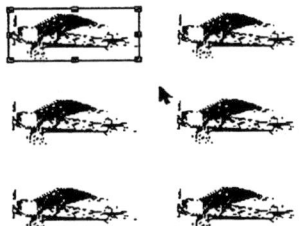

This difference can be demonstrated by the following exercise. Having imported the pictue of the plane, move it to the top left corner. Then use the Duplicate Many function to repeat the picture 2 across and 3 down with 2cm between them. We can then do something different to each one.

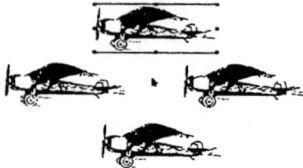

Now move the top four into the formation shown to the left. We can use this to demonstrate rotation by creating a 'loop-the-loop' picture. Select the one to the left. Then;

Move Mouse	(to Objects option on Menu Line)
Left-Click	Objects
Move Mouse	(to Rotate Object option)
Left-Click	Rotate Object
Dialog Box	'Rotate Objects' appears
Move Mouse	(to Rotate to Right)
Double-Click	Rotate to Right

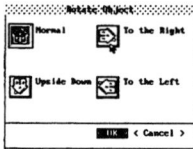

You will now see that the airplane is stood on its tail. Now follw the same procedure but choose upside-down for the top one and 'To the Left' for the one on the right. Move them about to see the loop properly. It should eventually look something like the illustration below;

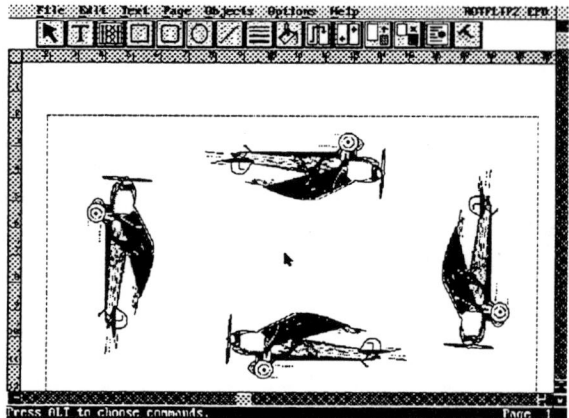

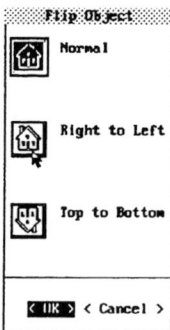

With Flipping, the process is basically the same except you have only two choice; to flip Left-to-Right and Upside-Down. Note that flipped upside-down and rotated upside-down are not the same. They face opposite directions. Use the bottom two airplanes to see the difference for yourself.

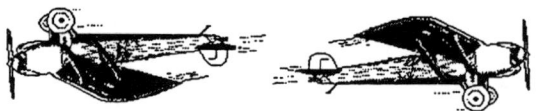

C7. Transparent and Solid Pictures

Pictures can also be modified in other ways. Making pictures solid or transparent can give you more freedom to combine pictures creatively.

Trophy.Tif
Opaque   Amerflag.Tif
Transparent

However, there are drawbacks. Firstly, EPDos2 only handles black-and-white images and putting two or more b+w images together often creates a complete mess. Secondly, putting an opaque image on top of another, you will see the border so there is no proper blend.

To test the effect of transparency and opacity, import the pictures 'AMERFLAG.TIF' and 'TROPHY.TIF'. Then try combining them in different ways. To change them from transparent to opaque and back you should follow the 'Object Specification' procedure detailed earlier in section B8. Left-Clicking the box marked 'Transparent' will alter the status of the picture.

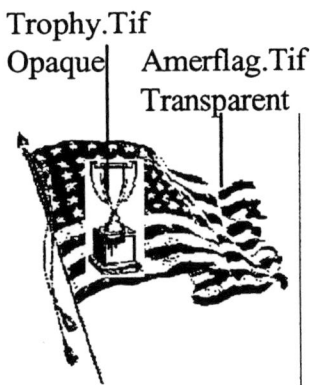

C8. Crop Image

World
Tree
Federation

Global
Conference
1992

London
Wembley
Conference
Centre

Some images imported may have parts that are useful and parts that do not fit in with your intentions. You can cut out or 'Crop' a lot of this extraneous detail. Similarly, you can crop a picture for creative effect.

To crop a picture, import the picture, 'TREES3.TIF' onto your page. Re-size it so it fills the screen better. Then;

Move Mouse	(to Objects option on Menu Line)
Left-Click	Objects
Move Mouse	(to Crop Image option)
Left-Click	Crop Image
Pointer	(becomes a pair of scissors)
Bottom Line	'Select a Picture to Crop' appears
Left-Click	(on 'Trees3.tif' image)
Bottom Line	'Press mouse button to select anchor point for cropping'
Move Mouse	(to where you want to start cropping)
Left-Hold	(hold button down)
Pointer	(changes to a cross)
Move Mouse	(to end of part to crop)
Bottom Line	(width and height shown)
Mouse	(release button)
Dialog Box	'OK to Crop' appears
Left-Click	< OK >

147

C9. Reversing Colours

For dramatic effect, you can turn a 'positive' image into a negative one, i.e., white becomes black and vice-versa. This is done by the Reversing Colours command. You must select a picture first, try ROSES.TIF, then;

Move Mouse	(to Objects option on Menu Line)
Left-Click	Objects
Move Mouse	(to Reverse Colours option)
Left-Click	Reverse Colours

The rose will now be a black rose

C10. Edit Bit Image

Cropping is a fairly gross way of modifying an image. You can do much finer alterations using the 'Edit Bit Image' feature in EPDos. This allows you to change every dot in a picture. The fish in this picture has gained a bubble and initials!

Unfortunately, you cannot edit all types of images. TIFFs, EPSs, and GIFs are excluded.

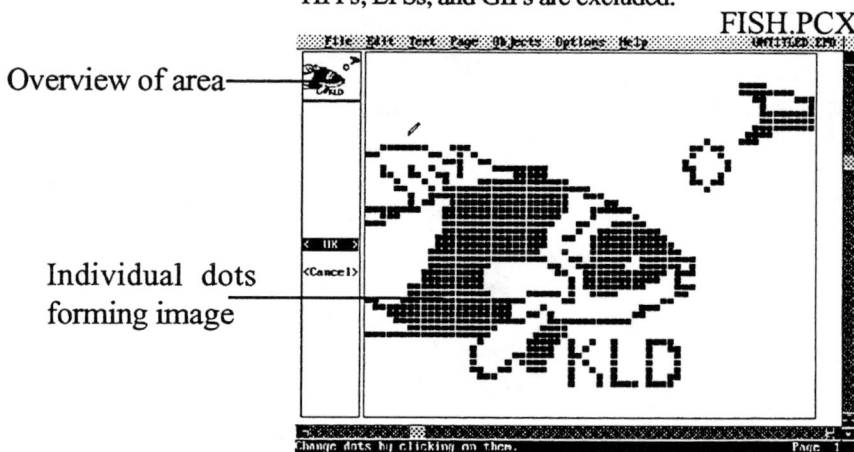

FISH.PCX

Overview of area—

Individual dots forming image—

All you need to do is import and select a picture, then;

Move Mouse	(to Objects option on Menu Line)
Left-Click	Objects
Move Mouse	(Edit Bit Image option)
Left-Click	Edit bit Image
Move Mouse	(to scroll bars)
Left-Click	(any pixels to change their colour)

Experiment to see how much effect small changes have.

148

C11.Saving as a Picture

Anything you create or modify in EPDos can be 'exported' out to a picture file in PCX format. For example, you might want to use the black rose created in C9 for other purposes. If you design your logo you may want to use that on all other documents you produce.

An example is the picture below that could be used for press adverts, in an author's societies newsletter etc.

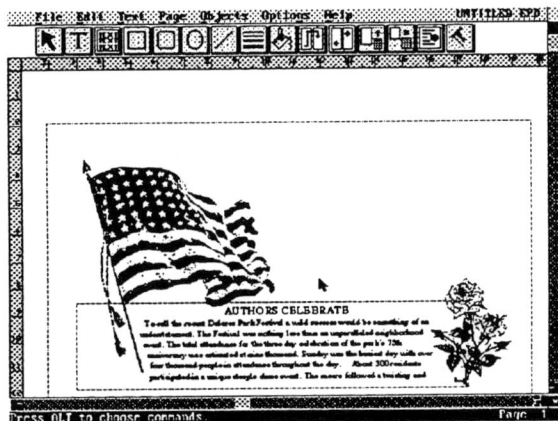

As an exercise, create a picture of your own combining text and pictures and a graphic. Then;

Move Mouse	(to File option on Menu Line)
Left-Click	File
Move Mouse	(to Save as Picture option)
Left-Click	Save as Picture
Bottom Line	'Draw a box around the area you wish to save as a picture' appears
Pointer	(changes to a cross)
Move Mouse	(to top left corner of whole picture)
Left-Hold	(hold button down)
Move Mouse	(to left and down to encompass whole of desired picture)
Dialog Box	'Save Picture' appears
Move Mouse	(to start of file name)
Type	(a new file name e.g. mypic1)
Left-Click	< OK >

You can now re-import this picture at any time you like as if an ordinary piece of clip-art. You can also modify it further in other graphics packages.

149

AUTHORS CELEBRATE

To call the recent Dolores Park Festival a wild success would be something of an understatement. The Festival was nothing less than an unparalleled neighborhood event. The total attendance for the three day celebration of the park's 75th anniversary was estimated at nine thousand. Sunday was the busiest day with over four thousand people in attendance throughout the day.   About 300 residents participated in a unique steeple chase event. The crowd followed a twisting and

Chapter 9.   The 'TextEffect' Package

A. Starting TextEffect   *152*

B. Features in Common with EPDos
    B1. The ToolBox   *153*
    B2. The Menus   *153*

C. The Text Manipulation Tools
    C1. Text Distortion   *155*
        Vertical
        Contoured
        Shadow
        Scaling
        Shear
        X-Scaling
    C2. Polygons   *157*
    C3. Curve Up and Curve Down   *158*
    C4. Distort   *159*
    C5. Rotate   *160*
    C6. Angle   *161*

D. An Exercise in TextEffect
    D1. The Aim of the Exercise   *162*
    D2. Exporting to Express Publisher   *162*

A. *Starting TextEffect*

TextEffect is not started like a normal program from DOS. Instead, it is launched from within EPDos. The way to do this is to move the mouse to the last icon in the ToolBox and double-clicking.

The screen will then change to the TextEffect screen as detailed in Section C of Chapter 2.

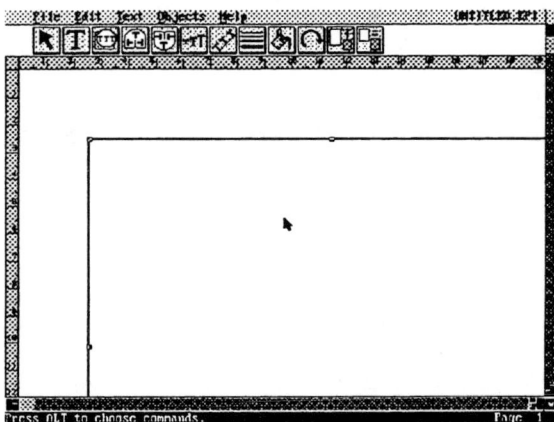

Most of its features are the same as in EPDos itself. The most notable difference is the absence of any text frame formatting ability. The simple reason is that TextEffect does not deal with framed text. It is designed to work with short phrases and single words that are manipulated to form logos, designs, headlines and banners.

This kind of text is sometimes referred to as 'Artistic Text' because the design is as important, if not more important, than the words used. It is the Effect of the Text that counts.

TextEffect allows you to do many text distortions and these can be used to make things leap out of the page at the reader. Don't bother using this facility for ordinary text, EPDos is perfectly capable of handling that.

The most important aspect of TextEffect is the freedom it gives you to experiment with different effects. This can be tremendous fun and this is the best way to approach using TextEffect. Treat it as a doodle-pad.

You can save the results in a separate file or incorporate them directly into your current document. It is usually better to do the former. It can't hurt and does give you that bit more flexibility.

152

B.   Features in Common with EPDos

B1.   The ToolBox

There are six icons common to both EPDos and TextEffect. These are the Pointer, Text, Set Line, Fill, Equate and Align features. However, they do not necessarily work the same in both programs.

A good example is the Text tool. In EPDos you simply start typing text onto the screen and into the frame. In TextEffect a Dialog Box appears and you type in your phrase and give it various characteristics. This limits the length of your phrase to a few dozen characters.

The Fill tool also changes as this now allows you to 'fill' the text. In other words, the strokes of the characters are filled with the chosen pattern if you wish. Letters are no longer confined to being a pure black but can adopt different shadings or densities. Larger characters can be given distinctive textures.

Furthermore, if you have put a shadow on the text, you can give this different fillings that adjust the effect from a heavy to a light shadowing

B2.   The Menus

The menus too are stripped-down versions of the EPDos ones but do work more or less the same.

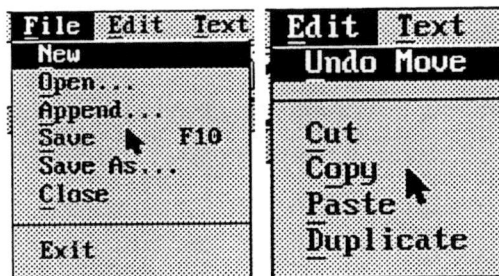

They have many less options. For example, in EPDos, the Text Menu has 12 options but only retains 4 in TextEffect. There are no Options or page Menus at all.

```
  Text  Objects  Help      Objects  Help
   Choose Font...           Bring to Front    CTRL+F
                            Send to Back      CTRL+E
   Justify Text..  ▶
                            Shuffle Up    ▶
   Kerning...               Shuffle Down
   Character Spacing..      Rotate Object...
                            Scale Object...   F9
```

```
  Help
   Using Help...
   Help Index...  ▶  F1
   Getting Started...
```

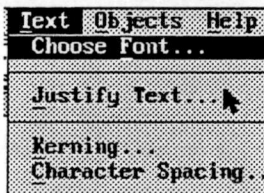

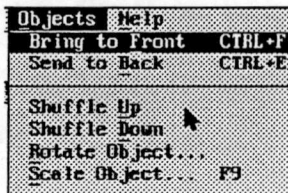

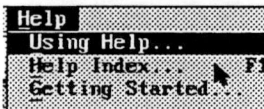

There is little point in detailing these options again with
the exception of one or two options such as Append and
Rotate Object. These are explained below.

C. The Text Manipulation Tools

C1. Text Distortion

Before entering TextEffect, draw a Box several cms wide and deep. With this Box still selected, double-click on the TextEffect icon. When the screen changes, you will find the Box is still there and still the same size. We will enter text into it and perform the basic text manipulations. Firstly, Left-Click on the second icon. The following Text Input Dialog Box will appear.

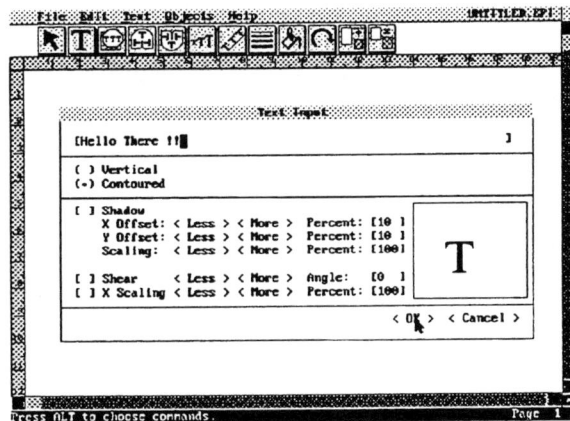

The choices available allow the text to be modified in various ways. The first choice is to decide if you want each character to be Vertical or Contoured. Choosing Vertical means that all the characters stand up regardless of whether they are fitted to a shape such as a curve.

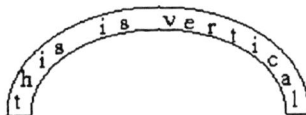

Contoured text, by contrast, has the characters at different angles to each other. With a half-circle, the first character would be flat on its back going through stood up straight and down to the last character being flat on its face. Contoured text more closely follows the path.

For this exercise, Left-Click the Vertical box. We will now try each effect in turn, adding to the previous ones. Start by typing in 'Hello There !!' on the text entry line. We shall modify this phrase repeatedly.

It should look like the picture to the left to begin with. None of the effects has been set. Before each change you must Left-Click the Text icon and after each one you should Left-Click the < OK > box.

Left-Click the Shadow [ ] to turn this effect on. Some of the values have already been set and these will apply.

Hello There !!

Now increase the X-Offset value from 10% to 30% by changing the number or Left-Clicking on the < More > box repeatedly (use the latter for small changes). The result is as below where the shadow has moved to the right. A negative value would shift it to the left.

Hello There !!!

Increase the Y-Offset by similar means from 10% to 30%. The shadow has moved down this time. A negative value would move it upwards.

Hello There !!!

The size of the shadow relative to the original characters can also be set. Change the Scale from 100% to 150% to make the shadow larger. A value below 100% would 'shrink' the shadow.

Hello There !!!

The characters can also be made to Shear or slant either forwards or backwards by a certain amount of degrees. Left-Click the Shear [ ] box and then change the value from zero degrees to thirty degrees. This will slant the text forwards or to the right whilst a negative value would make the text slant backwards or to the left.

Hello There !!!

Finally, turn the X-Scaling on by Left-Clicking the X-Scaling [ ]. This controls the thickness of the characters in the text line. The normal is 100% so change this to 50% so that each character becomes thinner.

C2. Polygons

Polygons are probably one of the least interesting of the TextEffect facilities. Basically, it allows you to produce a regular shape with between three and thirty sides and place a single line of text in the centre of it. Other text must be positioned manually.

Draw a roughly square box 5cm by 5cm in EPDos and then Left-Click the TextEffect icon. Once in, Left-Click the third icon along. The 'Polygon Sides' Dialog Box will appear on the screen.

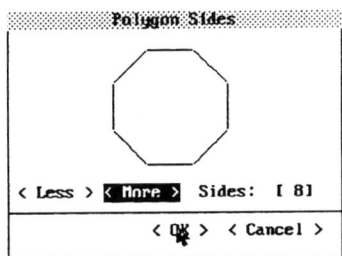

You can either repeatedly Left-Click the < Less > or < More > boxes or Left-Click on the Sides: [ ] box and enter the new number. Change it to eight and then Left-Click < OK >. An Octagon will now appear in the box.

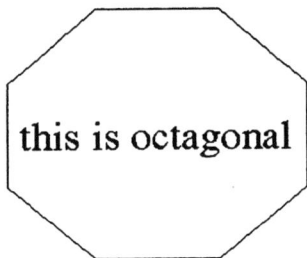

Now Left-Click the Text icon (second along) and type in 'this is octagonal'. Do not bother to change the other settings and the Contoured option has no effect. After Left-Clicking < OK > the following should appear.

this is octagonal

You can., of course, fill the box in and manipulate the text in the ways outlined above but it is not easy to make anything eye-catching from a polygon. Its best use is probably as part of a logo for your organisation etc. and mixed with other effects.

157

C3. Curve Up and Curve Down

Curving text is a very-eye-catching feature and one that many of the high-end DTP packages do not have and they cost 3-4 times as much ! You have the facility to curve text both up and down and from the slightly curved to the almost circular.

Text in a Curve Up reads left to right (clockwise) whereas in Curve Down the text still reads left to right but is anti-clockwise. Two half curves can be joined so that both lots of text read the correct way more easily. This is a common trick in logos and designs.

The illustration below shows what you can do with these simple but powerful effects. The only other effect used below is a Fill to demonstrate how other effects can be mixed and added in. Lines can, of course, be hidden.

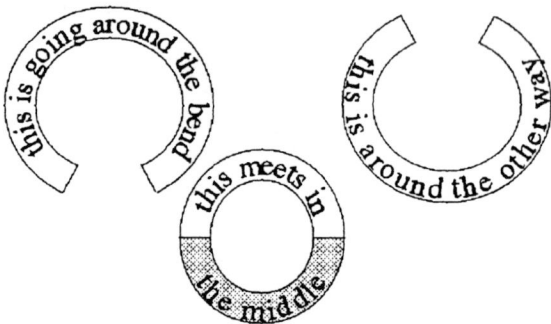

To use the curved text feature, enter TextEffect by Left-Clicking the last icon in EPDos. Then;

Move Mouse	(to fourth icon along)
Left-Click	Curve Down
Dialog Box	'Curve Angle' appears
Left-Click	([180] and then;)
Type	305
Left-Click	< OK >

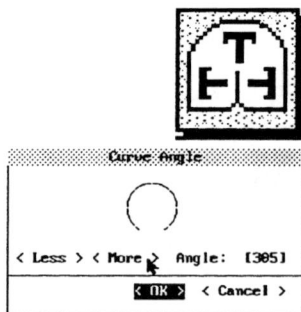

The Pen pointer will now appear and you should draw a square around 8cm by 8cm to give a circular appearance. If you make it taller then the effect will be more like a horse-shoe or magnet. Make it much wider and it will resemble a 'horse-collar'. If you Left-Click the < Less > or < More > options the angle will decrease or increase by 5 degrees each time.

158

A curve should appear like the one in the top left corner of the above illustration. Now;

Move Mouse	(to Text icon, second along)
Left-Click	Text
Type	this is going around the bend
Left-Click	( ) Contoured
Left-Click	< OK >

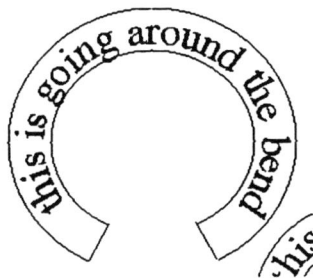

The curve with the contoured text should now resemble the top left-hand one. You can choose the Vertical option which will mean all characters stand upright. However, this does take up far more space and you will probably get an eror message saying that the text is too large and to choose another font size.

Alternatively, you could simply increase the size of the curve and if it is large enough then the text will flow around it automatically.

Now do the same exercise with the Curve Up feature and type 'this is around the other way'. The bottom figure in the illustration was created by making two 180 degree curves, one up and one down. Text was entered into each. The bottom one was then selected and Filled. They were then made the same size using the Equate icon. Finally, the two were moved together to appear joined. The process takes only a couple of minutes with practice.

Try the above exercise for yourself. Then experiment to your heart's content. Link semi-circles to create a 'Nessie' chain or make circles within circles. Have Fun !

C4. Distortion

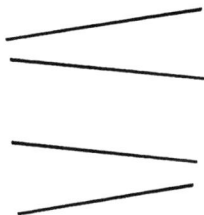

The Distortion feature allows you to give text a perspective which is either increasing or decreasing. Increasing perspective means that the first characters are small and successive ones become larger. With decreasing perspective, large ones to start with, shrink down.

The characters can be either vertical or be contoured and any other text feature such as shadowing and shearing can be added. However, the Distortion feature is not quite as good as it could be. The characters do not fill the shape out properly. Often this means that to achieve the right degree of distortion you must overdo the size of the box.

159

Using the Distortion feature is similar to the Curve one. With nothing selected in EPDos, Left-Click the TextEffect icon and then;

Move Mouse	(to sixth icon along)
Left-Click	Distortion
Dialog Box	'Distort' appears
Left-Click	Increasing
Left-Click	< OK >

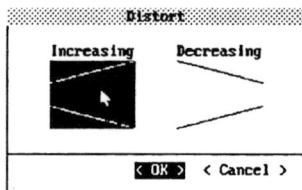

The Pen pointer will now appear and you should draw a frame approximately 8cm high by almost the width of the screen. In the frame should appear two diverging lines. You can drag the handles to change the size. Now;

Move Mouse	(to Text icon, second along)
Left-Click	Text
Type	text grows
Left-Click	( ) Contoured
Left-Click	< OK >

You can choose the Vertical option although this does take up far more space and you will probably get an error message saying that the text is too large and to choose another font size. You could simply increase the size of the frame and if it is large enough then the text will flow along it automatically.

text grows

As you can see, the growth is not exactly even and you may need to open the jaws wider to get the increase in size you require. When you have done this exercise, do the same again but choose the Decreasing perspective and add a few extra features to the text itself.

C5. Rotate

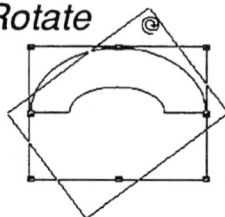

The Rotate tool is a fairly straightforward feature. You simply Left-Click the Rotate icon after which a Spiral pointer appears, select an object with it, and then rotate it as much as you wish.

160

C6. Line

at right angles

the mouse ran up the clock

This feature is poorly named. It does not create just a line as the name suggest but allows you to angle the text to any degree you wish. This means you can do all sorts of things as you will see from the simple example to the left.

An unusual feature of its use is that no Dialog Box appears. You simply Left-Click the seventh icon and the Pen pointer appears. Then you move the mouse to the first point where you Left-Click to anchor the line before moving to the next point where you want the line to end. For now, draw a line from the bottom left-hand to top right.

Now Left-Click the Text icon and type 'the mouse ran up the clock' before Left-Clicking < OK >. Then repeat the exercise drawing a line from the top-left to the bottom-right and typing 'at right angles' but remember to leave several spaces between the last two words.

D.   An Exercise in TextEffect

D1. The Aim of the Exercise

You should now set yourself an exercise in TextEffect. It is time to experiment. Think of an organisation or association or invent a fictitious company and design a new logo for them using the tools in TextEffect. Then try to incorporate this onto a letterhead and as part of a one-side newsletter or advertising flyer.

Try to use at least three or four of the TextEffect features and then export it to EPDos using the method below. The scale and shape of the logo will affect the use to which it is put. Graphic designers would normally produce 'Derivatives' for different uses. These are simply variations on the main theme used. You can use the Append option in the File Menu to bring a previous image back and add it to another image or amend it.

D2. Exporting to Express Publisher

It is always advisable to save the design before quitting TextEffect. This turns it into a form so that you can Import a Picture in EPDos and use the design like a Tif graphic file. Your design will normally be saved to the C:\EXPRESS\ART directory as an EPI file. From EPDos, you can then Save As A Picture in PCX format. This can be read by many other packages.

Chapter 10. Mixing Text, TextEffect and Graphics

A. The Objective
A1. The One-Page Advertising Flyer   164
A2. The Techniques Used   164
A3. Starting the Program   166
A4. Preliminaries   166

B. Creating the Banner in TextEffect
B1. Entering TextEffect   168
B2. Designing the Banner   168
B3. Exporting to the Normal Page   169

C. Entering the Text Frames
C1. Entering Dummy Text   170
C2. Formatting the Text   170
C3. Wrapping Text   170
C4. Adding Another Frame   171

D. Adding in Graphics
D1. A Simple Graphic Using the ToolBox   172
D2. Adding In Some Clip Art   172
D3. Positioning and Sizing   172
D4. Embedding , Sizing & Placing Graphics 173

E. Flowing Text Between Frames
E1. Linking Text Frames   174

F. Final Adjustmnents
F1. Removing Excess Lines   175
F2. Testing the Overall Effect   175
F3. Removing Dummy Text   175

A. The Objective

A1. The One-Page Advertising Flyer

An advertising flyer is often one page of A4 single-sided with both text and graphics used to promote the services of a particular company or organisation. Often they are referred to as 'junk-mail' which can be slightly unfair on the designer as he has almost certainly put a lot of effort in making something eye-catching and effective.

For the purposes of learning about DTP, the one-page flyer is ideal in that it allows you to combine nearly all the features of EPDos mentioned earlier. The next exercise is somewhat different to earlier ones in that it sets you an objective but does not specify every single step involved.

That is left purposefully vague to allow you to test your abilities. However, so that you do not feel completely abandoned, there is a good deal of guidance on the order in which to carry out the steps needed. The nearer you can get to the final result, the better you are doing.

As the exercise is only designed to demonstrate the steps involved, do not worry that the advert itself does not make sense. Often the wording would be altered to fit the design. This exercise only takes you to the end of the mock-up stage. You can put your own text in afterwards.

A2. The Techniques Used

The techniques used cover virtually every feature and technique you have practised before. These include;

Putting a shadow on text
Putting text on an angle
Using Curve Down
Using the Fill Feature
Saving TextEffect designs as pictures
Creating and filling text frames
Importing dummy text
Formatting text
Linking text frames
Drawing an ellipse
Importing graphic images
Wrapping text around pictures
Overlaying pictures and text
Moving and manipulating graphics

GLOBAL Graphic Designers of Britain Corporation

To call the recent Dolores Park Festival a wild success would be something of

an understatement. The Festival was nothing less than an unparalleled

neighborhood event. The total attendance for the three day

Serving Britain and every country. All around the Globe, on every continent and in every major metropolis !

celebration of the park's 75th anniversary was estimated at

nine thousand. Sunday was the busiest day

with over four thousand people in attendance throughout the

day. About 300 residents participated in a unique steeple

chase event. The racers followed a tortuous and treacherous

course around the edge of the park, entering at the

main concourse before a cheering crowd. The winner

was Peter Fensikoff, who works as a bicycle

messenger in the financial district. Clearly, the long

hours Peter spends riding up and down our steep hills

The cat sat on the mat and then the cat sat on the mat and then the cat sat on the mat and then the cat the cat sat on the mat and then the cat sat on the mat and then the cat sat on the mat and then the cat sat on the mat and then the cat sat on the mat and then the cat sat on the mat and then

The cat sat on the mat and then the cat sat on the mat and then the cat sat on the mat and then the

cat the cat sat on the mat and then the cat sat on the mat and then the cat sat on the mat and then

the cat sat on the mat and then the cat sat on the mat and then the cat sat on the mat and then

A3. Starting the Program

You should start EPDos in the normal manner. However, if you see a message saying that the memory is too low then you should exit the program and stop any others that operate in the background from working. You may be best advised to power down completely and start again.

A4. Preliminaries

Normally you would not have a clear idea of your design and nor would you be copying an already completed one. Therefore you would need to spend some time 'doodling' It is a good idea to use a pad of paper of the same size of the final result. It is no use drawing the design several times too large as it may not reduce well.

A small pad, however, may be useful for drawing the 'details' or elements of the final design. A good example is the banner usually found at the top of a flyer. You can use maximum creativity here to arrange and create the elements it contains and something eye-catching.

Many designers carry a small pad with them permanently as you never know when inspiration will strike next. When you are working on a project, this is a good example to follow, there is little worse than having a great idea on the bus home and being unable to remember it by the time you arrive home.

Try doodling the design on the previous page. Start with the banner, then the Footer. This gives the boundaries of your main design. Then draw a frame for the main text and where to put the graphics. Use simple outlines for text frames and graphics rather than detailed drawings. At this stage, balance is more important than accuracy.

You can also try different variations that may come in handy later on. When you have completed the exercise you can then try to alter to one of your own that you like better. Remember; design is a question of taste, there is no truly right or wrong result.

It is also important to remember that rough designs have a habit of changing when you come to do them for real. This might be because the computer system is incapable of making you design or because when you see it for real it is not as good as you imagined. The sketch on the following page shows how the design in the exercise started out. Compare this with the final result.

GLOBAL GRAPHICS DESIGNERS CORP.

Excellence In Effect

CURVED TEXT

B. Creating the Banner in TextEffect

B1. Entering TextEffect

Having started EPDos successfully, you should;

Delete the existing frame/border
Display a Grid using 1cm steps
Draw a Box from the top-left across and down

For this last step, we shall create our own co-ordinate system. Put the pointer (the Box tool one) in the very top left corner. This is 0,0. Now move across 1cm and down 1cm to position 1,1. Left-Hold the mouse button and move across to 20cm and down to 6cm. This is known as 20,6. Let go of the mouse button and you should have a Box from 1,1 to 20,6.

Enter TextEffect using its icon.

B2. Designing the Banner

The Banner consists of five main elements and we shall do each in turn starting with the word 'GLOBAL' which is on a slant and shadowed.

De-select the Box by left-clicking outside it
Draw a diagonal Line in the approximate position
Use the Text tool to enter 'GLOBAL' (in capitals)
Choose Contoured and Shadowed
Change the Font to Univers Med, 48-point, Bold, Italic
Set Line to Non-printing
De-select the text and line

Now repeat this to create the words 'Graphic' and 'Designers'. Next we need to create the word 'Corporation' using the Distortion tool.

Select the Distortion tool
Set it to Distortion Increasing
Use the Text tool to enter 'Corporation'
Choose Contoured and Shadowed
Do not change the font
Use the Rotate tool to make the baseline of the word level

The next step involves the use of the Curve Down and Fill features to create the 'of Britain' logo. Note that this is one piece that did change from the original doodle. The first attempt did not look as good as expected.

168

Select the Curve Down tool
Leave it at 180 degrees
Draw the curve frame
Use Text tool to enter 'of Britain'
Remove Shadow effect but leave Contoured
Use the Fill to give curve a light shading
Use Set Line to make curve outline non-printing

The banner is not basically set. However, it is unlikely that everything is in quite the right place so you should move each element around until you are happy that the positioning is correct.

You should now have the banner looking like below.

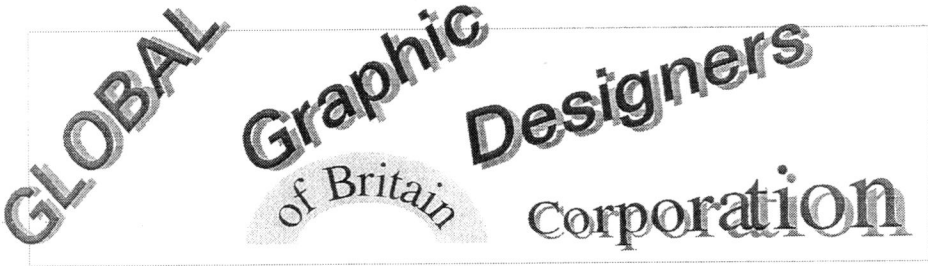

B3. Exporting to the Normal Page

You can take banners straight into EPDos but it is best to save them first, both in EPDos's own format and in the PCX format that can be transferred to other packages.

Use the Save option in the File menu
Save the banner as 'C:\EXPRESS\ART\BANNER1.EPI'
Exit from TextEffect and back to EPDos

In EPDos;
Delete original Box as it is no longer needed
Use Import As Picture to load banner
Place the banner in position
Use Save As Picture to put banner in PCX format
Save to a file called 'C:\EXPRESS\ART\BANNER1.PCX

Having got this section of the page correct, you should also save your 'work in progress'. To do this;

Use the Save option on the File menu
Call the file 'C:\EXPRESS\DOCS\FLYER1.EPD'

169

C.   Entering the Text Frames

C1. Entering Dummy Text

As discussed earlier, the text will often be the last item added in and so, for the time being, we will only add text that has been pre-prepared. It has nothing to do with the advertisement; it serves only to demonstrate the design.

Use the Text Frame tool icon
Draw a frame from 1,7 on the grid to 20,25
Use the Import Text option in the File Menu
Import file 'C:\EXPRESS\TEXT\AUTHOR.WPS

C2. Formatting the Text

The imported text is in the standard or default format and we want a different style altogether.

Delete the first text line
Select or highlight all the text in the frame
Use the Choose Font option in the Text menu
Select Helvetica Narrow, 18-point, Italic
Use the Justify Text option in the Text menu
Set justification to Full Justification
De-select the text

The text will now be significantly larger and the screen will appear horribly cluttered. Do not worry about this.

C3. Wrapping Text

Within the main text frame, there is another, smaller and filled one that would be used to emphasise or expand upon certain points. For example, it could contain a potted history of the organisation or a list of satisfied customers etc. The fill gives the text an added weight.

Use the Rounded Box tool
Draw a box from 14,18 to 19.5, 24.5
Use the Text Wrap icon in the Toolbox
Left-click the main text frame (which is to be wrapped)
Left-click the Rounded Box again
Use the Fill tool and select a light shading

The text from the frame should now flow around rather than under this new box. This stops text running into other pieces of text or graphics.

C4. Adding Another Frame

On top of this filled box you should now add some more text. Once again, the text needn't make any sense.

Use the Text Frame icon from the Toolbox
Draw a frame within the filled box.
Type 'the cat sat on the mat' repeatedly

You can use cut and paste to do the last step. Type 'the cat sat on the mat' once and then copy it. After that you repeatedly paste it until the box is filled.

To look at the work done, choose the Show Page option in the Page menu. Then save the work in progress to a file called 'C:\EXPRESS\DOC\FLYER2.EPD'.

To call the recent Dolores Park Festival a wild success would be something of an understatement. The Festival was nothing less than an unparalleled neighborhood event. The total attendance for the three day celebration of the park's 75th anniversary was estimated at nine thousand. Sunday was the busiest day with over four thousand people in attendance throughout the day. About 300 residents participated in a unique steeple chase event. The racers followed a twisting and treacherous course around the edge of the park, finishing at the main concourse before a cheering crowd. The winner was Peter Fensikoff, who works as a bicycle messenger in the financial district. Clearly, the long hours Peter spends riding up and down our steep hills helped him in his victory. Peter received a $100 gift certificate at Rainbow Grocery. Placing second and third were Brainderd Gondola, and Benjamin Melniyammer, respectively.

The Festival was conceived by Jane Joyce and James Austen, both longtime Dolores Park neighborhood residents. "We felt that neighborhood residents, as well as residents of the entire city, needed to become aware of the park's history," Jane said.

James continued, "We also thought that everybody should know not only about the park but the rich history of the Mission. It's amazing when you realize that just four blocks away on 16th is one of the oldest standing structures not only in San Francisco but in the State. It was getting people to be aware of that rich history and hopefully an appreciation for it that we first breached the idea of a park festival."

The cat sat on the mat and then the cat sat on the mat and then the cat sat on the mat and then the cat the cat sat on the mat and then the cat sat on the mat and then the cat sat on the mat and then the cat sat on the mat and then the cat sat on the mat and then the cat sat on the mat and then

D. Adding in Graphics

D1. A Simple Graphic Using the ToolBox

The Toolbox may not contain very high-powered graphics capabilities but what it has got can be used successfully to give a good effect.

To show this, we will add a circle containing text to the main text frame.

Use the Ellipse icon from the Toolbox
Draw a circle from 9,15 to 14,20
Use the Text Wrap tool (the wrap will be square)
Use the Text frame tool to make a frame
The frame must be slightly smaller than inside the circle

Then type the following; 'Serving Britain and every country. All around the globe, on every continent and in every major metropolis'. Typical Advertising Hype!

Use the Justify Text option in the Text menu
Centre Justify the text
De-select the frame and text

D2. Adding In Some Clip Art

As discussed earlier, EPDos comes with some Clip Art supplied. Other picture can be bought, particularly from shareware vendors who are very cheap compared to commercially available art libraries. For this flyer, we will simply use a couple of the images already available in the package. These are the trees and computer ones.

Use the Import Picture option in the File menu
Load in file 'C:\EXPRESS\ART\TREES3.TIF'
Place it on the left of the main text frame
Use the Text Wrap icon in the Toolbox

The wrap will flow the text around the shape of the tree

D3. Positioning and Sizing

Moving the tree around on the page will alter which bits of text flow and where. When you are happy then leave the graphic in position.

D4. Embedding, Sizing and Placing Graphics

The last graphic stood out from the text thanks to the use of text wrapping. This time we want a graphic that is mixed with or embedded in the text.

Use the Import Picture option in the File menu
Load in file 'C:\EXPRESS\ART\COMPUTR3.TIF'
Place it in the middle of the main text frame
Drag the handles to make it a much larger size
Place in the middle of the main text frame

The text should now flow over the picture of the computer. Being so large, the detail is not lost and neither is the text although having only black and white does limit the contrast and is something to be careful of.

To look at the work done, choose the Show Page option in the Page menu. Then save the work in progress to a file called 'C:\EXPRESS\DOC\FLYER3.EPD'.

To call the recent Dolores Park Festival a wild success would be something of an understatement. The Festival was nothing less than an unparalleled neighborhood event. The total attendance for the three day celebration of the park's 75th anniversary was estimated at nine thousand. Sunday was the busiest day with over four thousand people in attendance throughout the day. About 300 residents participated in a unique sack chase event. The racers followed a twisting and treacherous course around the edge of the park, which ended at the main concourse before arriving at The winner was Peter Popoff, who works as a bicycle messenger in the financial district. Clearly, the long hours Peter spends riding up and down our steep hills helped him in his victory. Peter received a $100 gift certificate at Rainbow Grocery. Placing second and third were Brandy Gondola, and Benjamin Melniyammer, respectively.

Serving Britain and every country. All around the Globe, on every continent and in every major metropolis !

The Festival was conceived by Diane Joyce and James Austen, both longtime Dolores Park neighborhood residents. "We felt that neighborhood residents, as well as residents of the entire city, needed to become aware of the park's history," Jane said.

James continued, "We also thought that everybody should know not only about the park but the rich history of the Mission. It's amazing when you realize

The cat sat on the mat and then the cat sat on the mat and then the cat sat on the mat and then the cat the cat sat on the mat and then the cat sat on the mat and then the cat sat on the mat and then the cat sat on the mat and then the cat sat on the mat and then the cat sat on the mat and then

E.   Flowing Text Between Frames

E1. Linking Text Frames

To see how linking text frames works, we shall use three text frames at the base of the flyer. For this exercise we shall call it the Footer (not strictly accurate but suitable).

Use the Rounded Box tool from the Toolbox
Draw a box from 1,26 to 20,29
Use the Fill tool and apply a light shading
Use Set Line to make line Non-printing

Use Box tool from Toolbox
Draw Box from 2,26.25 to 7,28.75
Draw Box from 8,26.25 to 13,28.75
Draw Box from 14,26.25 to 19,28.75

For each box, use Fill to make them white
For each box, use Set Line to make them Non-printing

We now need to create a text frame in each that we can then link together. To do and show this, highlight the whole of the 'The cat sat on the mat' text from the frame above where it was used previously.

Use the Copy option from the Edit menu
Select the first of the three frames
Use Paste to put the copied text into the frame

The copied text will now appear in the first frame but nothing in the second and third. A small bent arrow at the end of the first frame will indicate that there is more text to be placed. To do this;

Use the Text Link tool to link the first and second frames
Use the Text Link tool to link the second and third frames

The text should flow between each one now. Save to a file called 'C:\EXPRESS\DOC\FLYER2.EPD'.

The cat sat on the mat and then the cat sat on the mat and then the cat sat on the mat and then the	cat the cat sat on the mat and then the cat sat on the mat and then the cat sat on the mat and then	the cat sat on the mat and then the cat sat on the mat and then the cat sat on the mat and then

F.   Final Adjustments

F1.   Removing Excess Lines

The text in the main body is far to dense and instead of attracting the eye, it deflects it. Therefore, we need to thin the text out. EPDos does not have a built-in function for skipping lines of text so we shall have to do this manually.

This exercise also shows that the lack of a feature needn't necessarily stop you achieving it. With a little thought, you can often overcome the problem.

Left-Click the Text icon in the Toolbox
Move to the start of the second line of the main text frame
Press Return twice
Move down a line
Press Return twice

Continue these last two steps until there is a gap between every single line of text. The text will automatically re-flow around the graphics and text boxes with the exception of the embedded computer image.

F2.   Testing the Overall Effect

You should now be able to see the final result as shown on the next page. To look at the work done, choose the Show Page option in the Page menu. Then save to a file called 'C:\EXPRESS\DOC\FLYER4.EPD'.

If you wish to see a hard copy on paper, turn to Chapter 12 for details of how to do this.

F3.   Removing Dummy Text

Having seen that the design 'works' you would now change all the text to something more appropriate for the organisation. Try re-writing the main text, the filled-frame text and the footer text to promote the GLOBAL Graphic Designers Corporation of Britain'.

The text in the main body will be hard to edit as each text line is now effectively a paragraph. Be sure to type correctly first time. Alternatively, each line could be a complete sentence so that there is no link between each text line used.

Having achieve the desired result, you are now free to experiment with your own ideas so try a few.

175

GLOBAL Graphic Designers of Britain Corporation

To call the recent Dolores Park Festival a wild success would be something of an understatement. The Festival was nothing less than an unparalleled neighborhood event. The total attendance for the three day celebration of the park's 75th anniversary was estimated at nine thousand. Sunday was the busiest day with over four thousand people in attendance throughout the day. About 300 residents participated in a unique steeple chase event. The racers followed a long and treacherous course around the edge of the park, finishing at the main concourse before a cheering crowd. The winner was Peter Fensikoff, who works as a bicycle messenger in the financial district. Clearly, the long hours Peter spends riding up and down our steep hills

Serving Britain and every country. All around the Globe, on every continent and in every major metropolis !

The cat sat on the mat and then the cat sat on the mat and then the cat sat on the mat and then the cat the cat sat on the mat and then the cat sat on the mat and then the cat sat on the mat and then the cat sat on the mat and then the cat sat on the mat and then the cat sat on the mat and then

The cat sat on the mat and then the cat sat on the mat and then the cat sat on the mat and then the

cat the cat sat on the mat and then the cat sat on the mat and then the cat sat on the mat and then

the cat sat on the mat and then the cat sat on the mat and then the cat sat on the mat and then

Chapter 11. Creating a Complete Publication

A. The Objective
    A1. The Wizard - The Skydivers' Newsletter 178
    A2. The Techniques Used   178
    A3. The Preliminaries   181
    A4. Starting the Program   181

B. Creating the Banner and Footer
    B1. Creating a Simple Masthead Banner   182
    B2. Creating the Footer   182

C. Dividing the Page
    C1. Deciding Where to Place Dividing Lines   184
    C2. Making the Photo Box   186
    C3. Adding the Text Frames   186

D. Creating the Second Page
    D1. Creating a New Page   188
    D2. Creating the Sections   188
    D3. Adding Headlines   188
    D4. Drawing the Text Frames   189
    D5. Creating and Adding a TextEffect Logo   189

E. Adding the Text
    E1. Linking the Text Frames   191
    E2. Entering the Text into the Frames   191

F. Final Production Considerations   198

A. The Objective

A1. The Wizard - The Skydivers' Newspaper

The Wizard, used to illustrate a multi-page publication in this chapter, is a real newsletter produced for a real club. The club in question is a bunch of nutters called The Merlin Free Fall Club whose idea of fun is to hurl themselves bodily out of a speeding plane on freezing cold days. They then head down like a stone, doing a few acrobatics on the way, before commonsense prevails and they pull their 'chutes.

Steve White, the Wizard's editor, uses the newsletter to keep members both informed and amused. The layout is fairly straightforward and the equipment used is also relatively low-cost. It comprises a 386DX running at 25MHz, monochrome monitor, 65Mbyte hard disk, 4Mb of Ram and a Canon BJ10e Bubble-Jet printer. The total cost was less than £1000 brand new and the cost has fallen rapidly since.

The Wizard shows the standards that can be achieved using just simple equipment. However, without paying out large sums for equipment such as a scanner, some compromises are made. These include the logo of a diver and parachute being stuck on over the masthead banner. The space for the photographs is also left blank and a reduced photocopy of the original trimmed and pasted.

The final result is then photocopied and distributed amongst members. The results can be seen on the next two pages and this is a style that anyone should be able to emulate for their own use

A2. The Techniques Used

The techniques used cover many features and techniques you have practised before but less are used than for the advertising flyer. The ones used include;

Using Curve Down
Using the Fill Feature
Saving TextEffect designs as pictures
Creating and filling text frames
Formatting text
Linking text frames
Importing graphic images
Moving and manipulating graphics

178

THE WIZARD

Issue Number 9 - August 1992   THE MERLIN FREE FALL CLUB JOURNAL

Merlin Expands !

You will have noticed over the last few weeks that the tiny clubhouse at Topcliffe has become a giant sprawling metropolis. Dick Gays has installed the fan trainer (not quite bungee jumping but equally as scary by the look of it !) and the prefabs have arrived. The new extension will house a third lecture room, primarily for AFF and WARP instruction, and a rigging-room/store.

Room changes

This will allow Jan to use the old office for admin and the shop, and the manifest will move into the old AFF/WARP room. This will eventually have an outside door.

Help

Plenty of club members have been helping out with the work needed to make the extension look great. I've seen Fred, Gordon, Eleanor, Graham, Andy Tate, Kevin and most of the committee and instructors toiling away with the help of others too numerous to mention.I am sure there are still jobs for all you jumpers waiting for the weather - you don't need to be category 10 to wield a paintbrush !

Bad habits

The new layout of the clubhouse gives us the opportunity to change some bad habits. The packing area should be used for that and training first time courses. Please try to use the canteen for socialising. We hope to get some comfy chairs and more user-friendly tables. If you hang around the canteen you stand more chance of meeting newcomers to the sport who are just dying to listen to your "no shit, there I was" stories.

Progression Students Speak Out About Club

What do students think of club life ? Our roving reporter (alias the ed.) inveigled four students into talking to him one wet and very windy Sunday afternoon.

Matt Burman started jumping at Halfpenny Green but had to give up after three jumps. He later took up jumping again at Midland Parachute Centre and progressed to 5 second delays before joining Leeds University and discovering Topcliffe. His first impressions were of a very big club which seemed friendly and had a good atmosphere. Matt continued to progress and is now on tracks.

Waiting time is the main reason Matt feels that early students drop out of the sport. He has found the experienced jumpers willing to help but says that usually it is the student that has to make the first move. Matt thinks that we should have a door on the plane (whoever put that idea into his head ?).

On five second delays are Pauline Jack and Roger Goddard. They both did their first jumps here and have had broken progressions. Pauline stops for the winter (very wise !) and Roger has found that work commitments in the past have hindered his

continued on page 2 . . . .

Pie in your eye !

Nick gets the traditional treatment after his 100th jump

INSIDE : NEWS-p2   VIEWS-p3   UPDATES-p4

Record Free Fall

European skydivers have raised the world free-fall formation record to 150. Skydivers from 21 countries met in Belgium a few weeks ago. The 100 men and 50 women successfully completed a 150-way dive.

---

continued from page 1 . . . . .

progress. Both feel that more positive encouragement from experienced and club members would improve most students' progression. Pauline and Roger learned to pack because Bill Rule encouraged them. Most students are willing to help around the club too but do need to be asked.

Pauline says that the main reason she carries on skydiving is a mixture of adrenalin, fear and the challenge. Even bad jumps are worth it. Once again the weather features as a reason why students give up.

When the weather is bad there should be more for students to do. Perhaps we could build up a library of videos aimed more at the student market. A gripe about the clubhouse is the state of the women's toilet. Most women jumpers (and men for that matter) are willing to help keep the toilets clean - they just need someone to give them a push (or a brush).

Carl Blair trained at Merlin and is now on dummy pulls. The weather is a pain but he enjoys the sport so much it's worth the wait. The best place to meet is at the Red House.

Carl learned to pack to pass the time - he approached a club member and asked to be shown. He would like to see a faster turnaround of student lifts. Carl echoes Pauline and Roger in asking for there to be more things to do when the weather is bad (how about helping decorate the new extension ? - ed).

All ideas to the Wizard or committee.

Langar Boogie School

Two of our regular jumpers recently attended the Boogie School at Langar and have honed their already considerable free-fall skydiving skills. Steve Shaw and John Baggaley took time out from work and spent some time in Nottinghamshire in the company of other skydivers from around the world. The weather was kind to them and a great time was had by all.

John completed his 400th jump there, a two point 11-way. Later in the holiday he was in a successful two point 22-way. On arrival the jumpers joined one of two groups - a sequential group and the boogie school. Once the most incompetant jumpers had been binned, Steve and John did about 20 jumps, mostly 10- to 14-ways, organised by Rhino and filmed by Glen.

Snippets . . . .

Respect is due to Andy Tate who did his 600th jump at Peterlee with Eleanor, and Eleanor who did her 100th jump at Topcliffe with Andy Tate (Allan - eat your heart out !).
*****
Does anyone want to organise this year's xmas party? There is always someone willing to complain - but who is prepared to take over from the unsung heroine of xmas parties past, the indispensible Jan ?
If you are, see Jan...
*****
Does anyone fancy organising a competition ? This can be for experienced or student, accuracy, free-fall or whatever. Talk to Steve Thompson if you fancy it.
*****
Frapp hats can now be ordered through the club for £85 - see Jan.

Packing fees - anyone noticed how the static line rigs stay unpacked when there are free-fall rigs to pack, but it's always static line rigs we need more urgently. One club member has suggested we pay £3 for s/l and £2 for f/f. Comments ?
*****
.   Design a new t-shirt and get your name incorporated into the design - your chance for immortality. See Jan (it's true - Jan does do everything around here).
*****
Safety notice - There has been a recall for all type 17 (mini 1") main risers with RSL attached which were manufactured by Relative Workshop. See notice 2/92 on the board in the Packing Shed.
*****
Club's direct line: (0748) 875367.

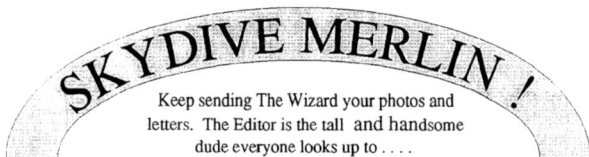

SKYDIVE MERLIN !

Keep sending The Wizard your photos and letters. The Editor is the tall and handsome dude everyone looks up to . . . .

A3. The Preliminaries

For this exercise, we shall only try to recreate the first two pages as they demonstrate everything you need to know. However, for the final result, try and find a picture in a magazine that will fit the size of the area allowed for the photograph and try to hand draw the logo used by Merlin.

Then, when you have finished as much work as is possible in EPDos, you can paste these down and photocopy them. You can also try adding your own pages 3 and 4 with your own invented stories and pictures. This will be good practice for you.

A4. Starting the Program

You should start EPDos in the normal manner. However, if you see a message saying that the memory is too low then you should exit the program and stop any others that operate in the background from working. You may be best advised to power down completely and start again.

B. *Creating the Banner and Footer*

B1. *Creating a Simple Masthead Banner*

Having started EPDos successfully, you need to create the Banner. In newspapers, these are sometimes referred to as 'Mastheads'. To create the Wizard one;

Delete the existing frame/border
Display a Grid using 1cm steps
Draw a Box from 1,1 to 20,3
Fill the Box with a light shading

Draw a Box from 1,3.5 to 20,4.5
Draw an oversized Text Frame from 1,3.5 to 20,5
Type 'Issue Number 9 - August 1992'
Tab several times
Type 'THE MERLIN FREE FALL CLUB JOURNAL'
Change Font to Times-Roman, 12-point, Plain
Pad out with spaces in middle to ensure fits frame

Draw largish Text Frame on left side of filled box
Type 'THE'
Change Font to Times-Roman, 48-point, Bold

Draw largish Text Frame on right side of filled box
Type 'WIZARD'
Change Font to Times-Roman, 48-point, Bold
Position and align both text frames with gap in centre

B2. *Creating the Footer*

The Footer is not a true footer but is used to tell the reader which section is on which page. It is fairly simple yet very effective in getting the message across.

Draw a Box from 1,26 to 20,27.5
Fill with a heavier shade than the banner
Set Line to Non-printing
Create a Text Frame larger than filled box
Type 'Inside : NEWS-p2   VIEWS-p3 UPDATES-p4'
Change the Font to Times-Roman, 24-point, Bold
Use spaces to set them apart properly

The page should now look like the one on the opposite page with just the masthead and footer.

Save as 'C:\EXPRESS\DOCS\WIZARD1.EPD'

THE   WIZARD

Issue Number 9 - August 1992   THE MERLIN FREE FALL CLUB JOURNAL

INSIDE : NEWS- p2   VIEWS-p3   UPDATES-P4

C. Dividing the Page

C1. Deciding Where to Place Dividing lines

The page now needs dividing up into sections for different articles and purposes. We have one tall column, a squarish one and a space for a photograph. Pictures on the front page are good at attracting attention. Remember the photographers' maxim; People Look At People!

To achieve some semblance of balance, we shall divide the page up into thirds and use a column one-third of page-width to act as the tall column. You could do this by eye and hand alone but we can calculate it as well.

The 'effective' page width runs from 1cm across to 20cm. This gives us 19cm. However, we want a gap between the text frames of 1cm so the figure goes down to 18cm. Fortunately, this divides nicely into three, i.e., 6 and 12.

To calculate the positioning of the tall text frame, add 6cm to the 1cm border at the edge of the page. It runs from 1cm to 7cm across. The other text frame is calculated by taking 12cm from 20cm to give 8cm. The dividing line, therefore, runs between the two at 7.5cm. Thus;

Draw a line from 7.5,5 to 7.5,26
Set Line to black and the finest line

To set the horizontal line position;

The boundaries run from 5cm down to 26cm, i.e., 21cm
Allow for 1cm gap between frames, i.e., 20cm
The result is 6.66cm and 13.34cm - Yuk !
Change this to 7cm and 13cm for easier line positioning
First frame boundary is 5cm+13cm, i.e., 18cm
Second frame boundary is 26cm-7cm, i.e., 19cm
Dividing line runs between them, i.e., 18.5cm

Draw a line from 8,18.5 to 20,18.5

This should now look like the page opposite with the masthead, footer and dividing lines.

Save as 'C:\EXPRESS\DOCS\WIZARD2.EPD'

THE   WIZARD

Issue Number 9 - August 1992   THE MERLIN FREE FALL CLUB JOURNAL

INSIDE : NEWS- p2   VIEWS-p3   UPDATES-P4

C2. Making the Photo box

The space for the photograph now needs reserving. Assuming you would normally photocopy and reduce a print and then paste it on the sheet before final copying, a solid black box has been used. The reason is that this overcomes several problems.

One is that a wavy or rough edge is not so noticeable. Another is that many prints have edges that fade out to near-white. This does not always come over too well if there is a lack of fine detail elsewhere. The solid black gives a definite border or edge (though this is not always so desirable). The border also makes the image stand out.

Steve White, Wizard editor and tall handsome dude (so he claims), sometimes uses an alternative method. This involves making a copy of the picture onto a Letraset Dot-Screen which is very good for fine contrast and reproduction on standard copiers. In this case, he would draw the box as a black line only and stick the Dot-Screen inside. This also overcomes the problem that many printers and copiers cannot handle full black very well.

To do the black-box method;

Draw a Square Box from 10,19 to 20,25
Fill with pure black
Set Line to Non-printing

This has left space for both a caption underneath and a headline to the left of the image.

C3. Adding the Text Frames

Draw Text Frame from 8,5 to 20,8
Draw Text Frame from 1,5 to 7,8

Type 'Merlin Expands'
Change Font to Helvetica-Narrow, 36-point, Bold
Select larger text frame
Type 'Progression Students Speak Out About Club'
Change Font to Helvetica-Narrow, 36-point, Bold

Draw Text Frame from 8,5 to 20,8
Draw Text Frame from 8,5 to 20,8

De-select text frames by clicking mouse outside them and then save as 'C:\EXPRESS\DOCS\WIZARD3.EPD'.

186

THE   WIZARD

Issue Number 9 - August 1992   THE MERLIN FREE FALL CLUB JOURNAL

Merlin Expands !

Progression Students Speak Out About Club

INSIDE : NEWS- p2   VIEWS-p3   UPDATES-p4

D. Creating the Second Page

D1. Creating a New Page

This is fairly straightforward and is done by;

Choose the New Page option from the Page menu
Choose the Blank option

D2. Creating the Sections

Using similar calculation methods to the earlier ones;

Draw a Line from 1,1 to 20,1
Draw a Line from 7.5,1.5 to 7.5,27
Draw a Line from 1,27.5 to 20,27.5
Draw a Line from 1,8 to 7,8
Draw a Line from 8,10 to 20,10
Draw a Line from 14,10.5 to 14,22

Save as 'C:\EXPRESS\ART\WIZARD4.EPD'

D3. Adding Headlines

This is a straightforward but repetitive process.

Draw a Text Frame from 1,1.5 to 7,2.5
Choose Font as Helvetica Narrow, 24-point, Bold
Type 'Free Fall Record'

Draw a Text Frame from 8,1.5 to 20,3
Choose Font as Helvetica Narrow, 24-point, Bold
Type 'Langar Boogie School'

Draw a Text Frame from 8,10.5 to 13.5,11.5
Choose Font as Helvetica Narrow, 18-point, Bold
Type 'Snippets'

Draw a Text Frame from 1,8.5 to 7,9.5
Choose Font as Helvetica Narrow, 14-point, Bold
Type 'continued from page 1 . . . .'

Draw a Text Frame from 8,26 to 20,27.5
Choose Font as Helvetica Narrow, 12-point, Plain
Type 'The views expressed are not necessarily those of
the committee or of the editor of The Wizard
Editor : Steve White'

Use tabs and spaces to get the postioning correct.

D4. Drawing the Text Frames

Now the ordinary text frames need adding. To do this;

Draw a Text Frame from 1,3.5 to 7,7.5
Draw a Text Frame from 8,3.5 to 20,9.5
Draw a Text Frame from 10,7 to 7,27
Draw a Text Frame from 8,12 to 13.5,22
Draw a Text Frame from 14.5,13 to 20,21

The last two frames need to be the same size exactly and so you will need to Equate them. Then Align them using the top left-hand choice in the set available.

Having done so, use the Show Page option from the Page menu to see the overall effect. See how it 'balances' well.

Save as 'C:\EXPRESS\DOCS\WIZARD5.EPD'

D5. Creating and Adding a TextEffect Logo

The 'SKYDIVE MERLIN !' logo on page two was created using the Curve Down tool in TextEffect. It is simple but acts as a skydiver's canopy quite nicely. This demonstrates that you do not need complex and detailed graphics in many cases.   Being appropriate is more important than being clever. To start with;

Draw a Box from 8,22.5 to 20,25.5
Left-Click the TextEffect icon
The Box transfers over
Use the Curve Down tool and keep it at 180 degrees

Unfortunately, the box is not deep enough as the curve only fills half the box frame. Therefore;

Double the depth of the Box
Left-Click the Text icon and type 'SKYDIVE MERLIN!'
Make sure the Contoured option is chosen
Fill the curve with a medium shading
Check Set Line is finest black
Save As 'C:\EXPRESS\ART\SKYDIVE1.EPI'
Exit TextEffect
Delete the original box
Import as Picture 'SKYDIVE1.EPI'
Place over position of original box
Save As 'C:\EXPRESS\DOCS\WIZARD6.EPD'

The result is shown overleaf.

Record Free Fall

Langar Boogie School

continued from page 1 . . . . .

Snippets . . . .

SKYDIVE MERLIN !

The views expressed are not necessarily those of the committee or of the Editor of The Wizard   Editor : Steve White

E. Adding the Text

E1. Linking the Text Frames

Firstly, some of the text frames need linking. Use F3 to jump to the first page. We shall link the text frame below the 'Progression ...' etc. headline to the lower part of the first column on the second page. To do this;

Left-Click the Link icon
Select the first frame to be linked
Choose Goto Page option and jump to page 2 (or just F4)
Left-Click lower frame in first column

Now any text typed in will flow from one frame to the other automatically. However, the frame on the first page does not have 'continued on page 2 . . . ' below it. This is the kind of thing you will spot when you proofread your own publication but it is good practice to go back and make corrections as you go along as well.

Press F3 to return to page 1
Create a small text frame below the main text frame
Type 'continued on page 2 . . . .'

You now need to link the two columns in the Snippets section on page 2.

Press F4 to jump to page 2
Choose the Link icon
Select frame below 'Snippets' and left-click it
Select frame to right of 'Snippets' and left-click
Save as 'C:\EXPRESS\DOCS\WIZARD.EPD'

The pages are now ready for your text to be entered.

E2. Entering the Text into the Frames

To enter the 'Merlin Expands !' story, select the text frame in the first column and type the four paragraphs (between the dotted lines) below after ensuring the font is Times-Roman, 10-point, plain and it is fully-justified;

. . . .

You will have noticed over the last few weeks that the tiny clubhouse at Topcliffe has become a giant sprawling metropolis. Dick Gays has installed the fan trainer (not quite bungee jumping but equally as scary by the look of it !) and the prefabs have arrived. The new extension will house a third lecture room, primarily for AFF and WARP instruction, and a rigging-room-cum-store.

Room changes

This will allow Jan to use the old office for admin and the shop, and the manifest will move into the old AFF/WARP room. This will eventually have an outside door.

Help

Plenty of club members have been helping out with the work needed to make the extension look great. I've seen Fred, Gordon, Eleanor, Graham, Andy Tate, Kevin and most of the committee and instructors toiling away with the help of others too numerous to mention. I am sure there are still jobs for all you jumpers waiting for the weather - you don't need to be category 10 to wield a paintbrush !

Bad habits

The new layout of the clubhouse gives us the opportunity to change some bad habits. The packing area should be used for that and training first time courses. Please try to use the canteen for socialising. We hope to get some comfy chairs and more user-friendly tables. If you hang around the canteen you stand more chance of meeting newcomers to the sport who are just dying to listen to your "no shit, there I was" stories.

. . . .

Always remember that you may not be able to get exactly the same as the illustration. Even very tiny differences in your text frames will cause changes. You may have to modify some of the text to fit it into the format. However, make sure you keep the meaning.

Now you need to type the following on the front page in the text frame below 'Progression Students. . . '. Ensure the font is Times-Roman, 12-point, plain (on page 2 you must reduce the size to 10-point to fit it in).

. . . .

What do our students think of club life ? Our roving reporter (alias the editor) inveigled four such students into talking to him one windy Sunday.

Matt Burman started jumping at Halfpenny Green but had to give up after three jumps. He later took up jumping again at Midland Parachute

Centre and progressed to 5 second delays before joining Leeds University and discovering Topcliffe. His first impressions were of a very big club which seemed friendly and had a good atmosphere. Matt continued to progress and is now on tracks.

Waiting time is the main reason Matt feels that early students drop out of the sport. He has found the experienced jumpers willing to help but says that usually it is the student that has to make the first move. Matt thinks that we should have a door on the plane (whoever put that idea into his head ?).

On five second delays are Pauline Jack and Roger Goddard. They both did their first jumps here and have had broken progressions. Pauline stops for the winter (very wise !) and Roger has found that work commitments in the past have hindered his progress. Both feel that more positive encouragement from experienced and club members would improve students' progression. Pauline and Roger learned to pack because Bill Rule encouraged them. Most students are willing to help around the club too but do need to be asked.

Pauline says that the main reason she carries on skydiving is a mixture of adrenalin, fear and the challenge. Even bad jumps are worth it. Once again the weather features as a reason why students give up.

When the weather is bad there should be more for students to do. Perhaps we could build up a library of videos aimed more at the student market. A gripe about the clubhouse is the state of the women's toilet. Most women jumpers (and men for that matter) are willing to help keep the toilets clean - they just need someone to give them a push (or a brush).

Carl Blair trained at Merlin and is now on dummy pulls. The weather is a pain but he enjoys the sport so much it's worth the wait. He found the club very big and daunting when he first came here, but says the best way to meet experienced jumpers is at the Red House.

Carl learned to pack to pass the time - he approached a club member and asked to be shown. He would like to see a faster turnaround of student lifts.

Carl echoes Pauline and Roger in asking for there to be more things to do when the weather is bad (how about helping decorate the new extension ? - ed).

Any ideas to the Wizard or committee.

The text should have automatically flowed onto page 2. Still on page 2, you should switch to the frame in the top left-hand corner and then type the following (in Times-Roman, 12-point, plain);

· ·

European skydivers have raised the world free-fall formation record to 150. Skydivers from 21 countries met in Belgium a few weeks ago. The 100 men and 50 women successfully completed a 150-way dive.

· ·

Now switch to the frame at the top right and use a font of Times-Roman, 12-point, plain and then type;

· ·

Two of our regular jumpers recently attended the Boogie School at Langar and have honed their already considerable free-fall skydiving skills.

Steve Shaw and John Baggaley took time out from work and spent some time in Nottinghamshire in the company of other skydivers from around the world. The weather was kind to them and a great time was had by all.

John completed his 400th jump there, a two point 11-way. Later in the holiday he was in a successful two point 22-way.

On arrival the jumpers joined one of two groups - a sequential group and the boogie school. Once the most incompetent jumpers had been binned, Steve and John did about 20 jumps, mostly 10- to 14-ways, organised by Rhino and filmed by Glen.

· ·

In the Snippets section, use Times-Roman, 10-point, plain and then type;

· ·

Respect is due to Andy Tate who did his 600th jump at Peterlee with Eleanor, and Eleanor who did her 100th jump at Topcliffe with Andy Tate (Allan - eat your heart out !).

*****

Does anyone want to organise this year's xmas party ? There is always someone willing to complain - but who is prepared to take over from the unsung heroine of xmas parties past, the indispensable Jan ? If you are, see Jan...

*****

Does anyone fancy organising a competition ? This can be for experienced or student, accuracy, free-fall or whatever. Talk to Steve Thompson if you fancy giving it a go.

*****

Packing fees - anyone noticed how the static line rigs stay unpacked when there are free-fall rigs to pack, but it's always static line rigs we need more urgently. One club member has suggested we pay £3 for s/l and £2 for f/f. Comments ?

*****

Design a new t-shirt and get your name incorporated into the design - your chance for immortality. See Jan (it's true - Jan does do everything around here).

*****

Safety notice - There has been a recall for all type 17 (mini 1") main risers with RSL attached which were manufactured by Relative Workshop. See notice 2/92 on the board in the Packing Shed.

*****

Club's direct line: (0748) 875367.

. . . .

Now draw a text frame below the 'SKYDIVE MERLIN!' logo and fill it with the following in Times-Roman, 12-point, Plain and centre-justified.

. . . .

Keep sending the Wizard your photos and letters. The editor is the tall handsome dude that everyone looks up to...

. . . .

All that remains is to return to the first page and create two text frames; one for the caption under the photo area and one at the side of it.

Save as 'C:\EXPRESS\DOCS\WIZARD8.EPD'

The result should look like the illustration on the next two pages. If you want, you can now use a variation on the theme used to produce your own pages 3 and 4 and make up your own articles and graphics.

THE WIZARD

Issue Number 9 - August 1992

THE MERLIN FREE FALL CLUB JOURNAL

Merlin Expands !

You will have noticed over the last few weeks that the tiny clubhouse at Topcliffe has become a giant sprawling metropolis. Dick Gays has installed the fan trainer (not quite bungee jumping but equally as scary by the look of it !) and the prefabs have arrived. The new extension will house a third lecture room, primarily for AFF and WARP instruction, and a rigging-room/store.

Room changes

This will allow Jan to use the old office for admin and the shop, and the manifest will move into the old AFF/WARP room. This will eventually have an outside door.

Help

Plenty of club members have been helping out with the work needed to make the extension look great. I've seen Fred, Gordon, Eleanor, Graham, Andy Tate, Kevin and most of the committee and instructors toiling away with the help of others too numerous to mention.I am sure there are still jobs for all you jumpers waiting for the weather - you don't need to be category 10 to wield a paintbrush !

Bad habits

The new layout of the clubhouse gives us the opportunity to change some bad habits. The packing area should be used for that and training first time courses. Please try to use the canteen for socialising. We hope to get some comfy chairs and more user-friendly tables. If you hang around the canteen you stand more chance of meeting newcomers to the sport who are just dying to listen to your "no shit, there I was" stories.

Progression Students Speak Out About Club

What do students think of club life ? Our roving reporter (alias the ed.) inveigled four students into talking to him one wet and very windy Sunday afternoon.

Matt Burman started jumping at Halfpenny Green but had to give up after three jumps. He later took up jumping again at Midland Parachute Centre and progressed to 5 second delays before joining Leeds University and discovering Topcliffe. His first impressions were of a very big club which seemed friendly and had a good atmosphere. Matt continued to progress and is now on tracks.

Waiting time is the main reason Matt feels that early students drop out of the sport. He has found the experienced jumpers willing to help but says that usually it is the student that has to make the first move. Matt thinks that we should have a door on the plane (whoever put that idea into his head ?).

On five second delays are Pauline Jack and Roger Goddard. They both did their first jumps here and have had broken progressions. Pauline stops for the winter (very wise !) and Roger has found that work commitments in the past have hindered his

continued on page 2 . . . .

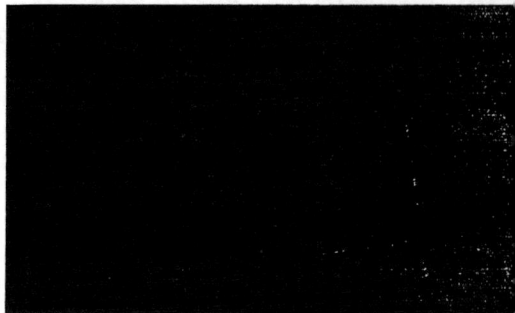

Record Free Fall

European skydivers have raised the world free-fall formation record to 150. Skydivers from 21 countries met in Belgium a few weeks ago. The 100 men and 50 women successfully completed a 150-way dive

continued from page 1 . . . . .

progress. Both feel that more positive encouragement from experienced and club members would improve most students' progression. Pauline and Roger learned to pack because Bill Rule encouraged them. Most students are willing to help around the club too but do need to be asked.

Pauline says that the main reason she carries on skydiving is a mixture of adrenalin, fear and the challenge. Even bad jumps are worth it. Once again the weather features as a reason why students give up.

When the weather is bad there should be more for students to do. Perhaps we could build up a library of videos aimed more at the student market. A gripe about the clubhouse is the state of the women's toilet. Most women jumpers (and men for that matter) are willing to help keep the toilets clean - they just need someone to give them a push (or a brush).

Carl Blair trained at Merlin and is now on dummy pulls. The weather is a pain but he enjoys the sport so much it's worth the wait. The best place to meet is at the Red House.

Carl learned to pack to pass the time - he approached a club member and asked to be shown. He would like to see a faster turnaround of student lifts. Carl echoes Pauline and Roger in asking for there to be more things to do when the weather is bad (how about helping decorate the new extension ? - ed).

All ideas to the Wizard or committee.

Langar Boogie School

Two of our regular jumpers recently attended the Boogie School at Langar and have honed their already considerable free-fall skydiving skills. Steve Shaw and John Baggaley took time out from work and spent some time in Nottinghamshire in the company of other skydivers from around the world. The weather was kind to them and a great time was had by all.

John completed his 400th jump there, a two point 11-way. Later in the holiday he was in a successful two point 22-way. On arrival the jumpers joined one of two groups - a sequential group and the boogie school. Once the most incompetant jumpers had been binned, Steve and John did about 20 jumps, mostly 10- to 14-ways, organised by Rhino and filmed by Glen.

Snippets . . . .

Respect is due to Andy Tate who did his 600th jump at Peterlee with Eleanor, and Eleanor who did her 100th jump at Topcliffe with Andy Tate (Allan - eat your heart out !).
*****
Does anyone want to organise this year's xmas party? There is always someone willing to complain - but who is prepared to take over from the unsung heroine of xmas parties past, the indispensible Jan ?
If you are, see Jan...
*****
Does anyone fancy organising a competition ? This can be for experienced or student, accuracy, free-fall or whatever. Talk to Steve Thompson if you fancy it.
*****
Frapp hats can now be ordered through the club for £85 - see Jan.

Packing fees - anyone noticed how the static line rigs stay unpacked when there are free-fall rigs to pack, but it's always static line rigs we need more urgently. One club member has suggested we pay £3 for s/l and £2 for f/f. Comments ?
*****
.   Design a new t-shirt and get your name incorporated into the design - your chance for immortality. See Jan (it's true - Jan does do everything around here).   .
*****
Safety notice - There has been a recall for all type 17 (mini 1") main risers with RSL attached which were manufactured by Relative Workshop. See notice 2/92 on the board in the Packing Shed.
*****
Club's direct line: (0748) 875367.

SKYDIVE MERLIN !

Keep sending The Wizard your photos and letters. The Editor is the tall and handsome dude everyone looks up to . . . .

The views expressed are not necessarily those of the committee or of the Editor of The Wizard   Editor : Steve White

F. *Final Production Considerations*

For the truly final result, you will need a pair of scissors and some 'Magitape' or Pritt which are ideal for sticking photographs and hand-drawn logos down onto the master sheets for photocopying.

Another possibility to consider is to use an A3 copier and putting sheets 1 and 4 together on one side and 2 and 3 on the other in order to create a publication that opens up. This is much better than a stapled or loose one.

The Wizard Logo

Pie

in

your

eye !

Nick gets the traditional treatment after his 100th jump

Chapter 12. Printing Documents

A. **The Issues Involved**
A1. Printer Connections   200
A2. The Speed of Your Printer   201
A3. High and Low Resolutions   201
A4. Draft and Final Output   202
A5. Fonts Supported   202
A6. Printer Margins   202
A7. Using a Copier   202

B. **Printing Options**
B1. Choosing a Printer   203
B2. The Print Options   204
B3. The Options Available   204

A. The Issues Involved

Whilst you were learning to use DTP and EPDos, you probably consumed much caffeine. Be warned! You are now entering another potential coffee minefield.

For some strange reason, many experienced computer uses find their encounters with getting computers and printers to work together tend to fall into one of two categories; the sublime and the ridiculous. Admittedly the situation has improved over the years but it is still possible to spend an incredible amount of time poring over PC, printer and software manuals.

If you already have a printer then this will be academic to you. If not, then read this section very carefully before making any choices and spending any cash.

A1. Printer Connections

There are two basic types of printer connection available and most printers have only one or the other although some do have both.

The most popular type is the Parallel printer. The reasons for its success are that it is simple and reliable. Assuming both PC and printer have parallel ports, this is as near a plug-in-and-go device as you are likely to find. Often a parallel port is denoted as LPT1 (or some other number).

Many older printers, and dot-matrices in particular, use a Serial port. They are much trickier to handle and often requires the changing of many fiddly little switches and an appreciation of computer communications ! Buy a new jar of coffee. Serials are denoted as COM1 etc.

The moral of this section is that nine out of ten DTPers prefer parallel ports. You know it makes sense.

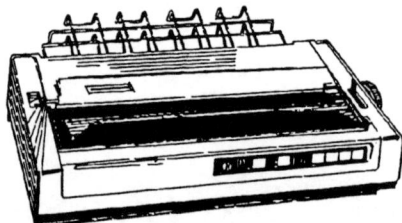

A2. The Speed of Your Printer

The first rule of estimating printing times is to ignore completely and utterly everything the printer blurb or manual says. An easy rule of thumb is to halve all claimed speed ratings. These quotes are based on an 'ideal' document, i.e., one that makes the printer appear better than it is.

Whilst this is true of printing normal word-processed documents. When it comes to DTP and graphics the timings and speeds are utterly wrong. This is as true of a £1000 laser as it is a £100 Dot-matrix.

You can buy hardware devices called Print Spoolers but these are largely a waste of money unless you are concerned with squeezing out every extra ounce of speed. They are basically boxes of memory chips

Some printers have memory stores that can be added to if necessary. In dot-matrix printers this is often referred to as a buffer and is effect for text but less so for graphics. The more complex the print job the less effective one is.

In laser printers, the memory can often be increased by either a memory board or an add-in cartridge (basically a board in a casing). The standard 0.5Mbyte memory will suffice for many text-based jobs but will really stall on graphics. If you face problems then add a couple of MBytes to give the speed a boost.

A3. High and Low Resolutions

EPDos allows you to choose between High Resolution and Low Resolution printing. Measured in Dots Per Inch, the 300DPI setting is considered top quality printing for lasers, 150DPI is medium and 75DPI is low quality. Of course, these really only apply to lasers and bubble-jets,

The options you are given depend on the printer you are ausing and have set up for use via the 'Choose Printer' command. You may be given options of 360, 180 and 60 DPI instead. However, with a dot-matrix, the printer will only be able to use its normal 9 or 24 pins and try to approximate the real thing.

A4. Draft and Final Output

One strategy commonly adopted to speed up production of a document is to print the development copies in low resolution or Draft form and only print the Final or most important versions in top quality mode. You can also reeserve space for pictures and graphics but not fill them in until the last minute.

A5. Fonts Supported

If you are using anything other than a PostScript printer you will only be able to use the fonts that are held in the printers own memory. However, these do print very fast. The fonts may not appear exactly as they seem on the screen and with some printers one font is entirely substituted for another although the space used is the same.

A6. Printer Margins

These margins, as opposed to Page Margins, refer to the non-printing border on an A4 sheet put through a bubble jet or laser. It is usually less than a centimetre on each side plus top and bottom although colour printers may be worse than this. You must allow for this in your design.

A7. Using a Copier

As mentioned in the earlier chapter, one of the best ways to produce multiple copies quickly, especially ones using lots of graphics, is to use a photocopier. This means that it is vitally important to have as good a 'master' copy as possible. Some people reserve high quality paper and fresh ribbons or toner cartridges especially for these. Other copies are printed using any old materials.

B.   Printing Options

B1.   Choosing a Printer

When you set up EPDos, you chose one or more printer 'drivers' to be installed. You can now select from these the printer you are currently using. Each driver may allow more than one model of printer to be used and some printers can emulate or pretend to be other makes.

Some makes such as Hewlett-Packard and Epson tend ot be industry leaders and other, lesser-known or unbranded printers may state 'Compatible with Epson LQ-850' or 'LaserJet II Emulation. These are the driver you should have installed and now be able to choose from. E.g.,

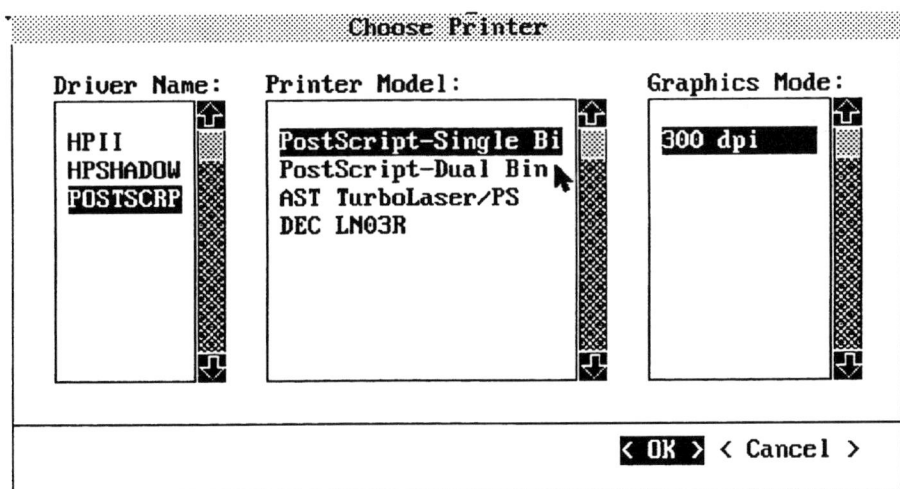

In this case three printers were installed. A Hewlett-Packard LaserJet II, the same again with the overlapping objects or Shadow feature used and a PostScript driver.

The latter has been chosenn and four printers have been listed. The first two are generic and almost any PostScript will conform to these. The latter are modified versions. The standard one has been selected. There is only one option for print quality.

If the other drivers had been chosen there would have been more choices.

B2. The Print Options

Having made sure the correct printer driver has been selected, and that all connections are sound, it is time to print. Choosing the Print option from the File menu, the Dialog Box below will appear.

```
      Print to PostScript-Single Bin (300 dpi)

  Number of Copies: [1 ]
  [X] Print specific pages: [1-5,7,15-11█  ]
  [ ] Manual paper feed

  (•) Printer at Lpt1      ( ) Printer at Com1
  ( ) Printer at Lpt2      ( ) Printer at Com2
  ( ) Printer at Lpt3      ( ) Printer at Com3
  ( ) Printer at Lpt4      ( ) Printer at Com4
  ( ) Disk Printer File
  ( ) DCX File
  ( ) Intel Connection CoProcessor (facsimile/file output)
  ( ) ASCII text file (Document text export)

                              < OK >   < Cancel >
```

Note that the top line shows the printer chosen before.

B3. The Options Available

The first option to consider is how many copies you want printing (up to 99).

You can then choose the precise pages you want to print. In the example above, pages 1,2,3,4,5,7,15,14,13,12,11 will be printed in that order. Left click the Check box.

Manual paper feed should be left-clicked only when you are using single sheets by hand rather than using continuously-joined or automatically-fed sheets of paper

The next block allows you to send the print job to either a parallel (LPT) or serial (COM) printer. The number depends on the configuration of your PC but 1 is normal.

You are unlikely to use the last three but the Disk Printer File option can be useful. You could send the print job to a floppy disk file which can then be copied and sent to others to print to their own printer using the Dos command; COPY /B WIZARD1.PRN LPT1 (or similar).

204

Chapter 13. Designing Your Own Publications

A. DesignIdeas
    A1. Magazines
    A2. Newspapers
    A3. Books
    A4. Leaflets and Brochures

B. Good Reading - The Best DTP Books

C. Rules of Layout
    C1. The Rough Guide to Rules
    C2. Making and Breaking
    C3. Good Authoring

A. DesignIdeas

Good design ideas are all around you. You don't need to look far, only visit your local newsagent or go into any town centre and browse the shelves of the big newsagents and bookstores. If your budget is limited, you can always ask your local doctor or dentist to save you some magazines rather than throw them out.

A1. Magazines

No matter what you are using DTP for, there is likely to be some magazine related to the subject. The main consumer magazines generally work on the principle that the design is as important as the information.

An eye-catching front-page is essential in the circulation war raging on every news-stand shelf.. The essence of the front-page is to show the potential buyer that the magazine has what he or she wants between the covers by firstly being attention-grabbing and secondly highlighting the most interesting or exciting features inside.

In a sense the front is 'obvious and comfortable'. Women's magazines and TV guides go for big names rather than trying to promote more worthy causes. Photographic magazines either use a woman's face and figure or go for a large, single bright object firmly in the centre.

House and Home magazines use large and beautiful spreads while county magazines aim for a more relaxed and parochial look achieved by using less modern font and photographs that do not leap out at you.

By an ironic twist, this can mean that certain magazines go out of their way to be as obscures as possible but that too can attract a certain audience. For example, magazines dealing with the fringes of science can use almost incomprehensible pictures. To someone with an inquiring mind this can act like a magnet.

The importance of magazine to the budding DTPer is that they teach you to focus on your potential audience. Any publication based purely on your own likes and dislikes will be doomed to failure. Unless you try to take into account what your potential readers want, be they a captive audience or otherwise, then all your hard effort will be wasted. Don't let your work end up in the bin, try to ensure people actively look forward to its arrival.

A2. Newspapers

Sadly, national newspapers in Britain pander too much towards people prejudices and fall into one of two classes. The first is the 'Broadsheet' or large folded format heavyweight papers that are long on analysis but generally lacking accessibility. The second is the 'Tabloid' or small format that substitutes sensation for substance.

Attempts have been made at bridging the divide but these have not generally lasted long. The consensus seems to be that people do not want their view of the world challenging over the cornflakes.

If newspapers have any value for the DTPer it is that they take a story or article and break it into manageable chunks. Paragraphs are no more than a couple of inches long and sentences are normally 15-20 words long. Graphics are often used to illustrate something not easily translated or conveyed in words.

The page layout varies from section to section and within a page there are small sections and stories do not just go top to bottom, left to right. Headlines are used to grab attention whilst the first paragraph is used to explain the story and draw the reader further in.

The main regional dailies are the nearest Britain has to a reasonable balance of information and interest. Whilst often dismissed as parochial, they do understand their local population as is evident from the sales they achieve from an essentially limited catchment area.

They often take national issues and bring the focus nearer home to a level people can relate to. After all, the redundancy of a few 'Champagne Charlies' in the City may be treated with derision and even glee by most but it is a different story when the redundancies detailed are on your own doorstep.

Small town newspapers are generally less than exciting though there are a few good exceptions. Most of the local populace will appear in their pages three times (their birth, marriage and death).

However, their scale and ambitions are probably more in line with those of the novice DTPer. The challenge is to be as attention-grabbing as the nationals, as focused as the provincials and on the scale of the locals.

A3. Books

Paperback books are generally page after page of 'square' and are of little relevance to the DTPer unless they have some graphic design content which is rare. There is little in most paperbacks lack could not be set on a good word-processor. The same is true of hardback novels.

More useful are the instructional books such as d-i-y or hobby ones as these use graphics and text to illustrate particular points. Both the content and the style are more akin to the normal home DTPer's interests.

The so-called 'coffee-table' books (ironic given DTP's high caffeine factor) are of only limited value although some are just like large scale versions of the instructional books. However, most rely on large-format, glossy photographs for effect; something you won't be able to emulate on home equipment.

A4. Leaflets and Brochures

Junk mail can be a valuable resource to the DTPer. It is free and readily available. These leaflets are designed to catch the eye and entice you to buy. They come in all shapes and sizes and it is worth keeping a file of all the ones you find most interesting and appropriate to your use of Desk Top Publishing.

Getting hold of brochures for all kinds of goods and services is usually quite easy. They either come through your letter-box or you phone or write off for one. Brochures also major one good layout.

Other forms of leaflet come at you from left and right. Government departments produce them by the bucket-load and some of them are even quite good. They have learnt over the recent years that just giving the information is only part of the process; you have to make sure people can understand it fully.

Post Offices are also a good source of designed leaflets and most big organisations are only too happy to give out information sheets.

The trick for all these sources is that when you see a good piece of design or well-presented information, keep it for those periods when your brain seizes up and the caffeine fails to stimulate the brain cells; just glance through your 'Ideas' files until the cogs start to turn again.

B.   Good Reading - The Best DTP Books

Assuming you enjoy DTP, and if you've managed to get this far then you should do, then you may want to extend your skills and knowledge beyond the scope of an introductory book such as this.

There are many books available ranging from the simple to the heavyweight. However, most are dedicated to a particular software package and as such are largely useless to you. Fortunately, there are some that are not so heavily slanted and could be of use to the EPDos user.

This section gives you a list of the most commonly available ones and a brief guides as to how useful they are likely to be to you. None are outright bad but this book may have covered much of the same ground. Even so, most books will still contain some things of value to you so borrowing through a library is a good idea. Others are worth buying for hard cash.

'Into Print'

Having learnt the skills needed for DTP and how to use EPDos, you may want to scale-up production. This book looks less at DTP technique and more at methods of production and even at costings. This could be of great use to individuals and organisations of limited means.

Real people's experiences are used as examples of the way DTP is used. This would also make a good teaching resource for lecturers and trainers.

There is a limited look at layout design and a short review of the major packages but its main drawback is the amount of emphasis on Mac software and may be more appropriate for full-time DTPers. However, the book is easy to read, lightly-styled and humorously illustrated.

Authors   :   Susan Quilliam/Ian Grove-Stephenson
Published   :   B.B.C. Books
Price   :   Around £9

'Desktop Publishing Secrets'

In the US , a magazine has been going for many years called Publish! and this has always been a fount of knowledge for the DTP brigade. This book is a distillation of many of the articles it has featured in recent years and is a goldmine of information.

Its main strength is that it details the tricks of the trade for achieving effects that are not necessarily built-in to a particular package. Many of these can be applied to other packages which lack the same feature. Special effects such as these can help your work stand out.

This is a fairly heavyweight book and is aimed at the advanced and demanding user or enthusiast. The drawback is that it concentrates on the top-end packages but its most important message is that if there's a will there's a way around a problem.

Authors	:	Eckhardt, Weibel, Nace
Published	:	Peachpit Press
Price	:	Around £25

'Collier's Rules for Desktop Design and Typography'

This is an extremely useful book for anyone using a lot of text in their publications or who is just fascinated by type styles and typography. It shows the rules as well as how and when to break them.

It is glossy and has excellent illustrations but is maybe a little too flashy and crowded. If you are likely to be sending materials to a printer or typesetter, then it will also help you understand and speak the same language.

Authors	:	David Collier
Published	:	Addison-Wesley
Price	:	Around £15

'Looking Good In Print'

This is a must-have for the serious DTP users. It is not about individual packages but about design; what looks good, bad and indifferent. It concentrates on what works and what is a waste of space.

This is a 'heavyweight' book in all senses of the word BUT DO NOT LET THIS PUT YOU OFF! The information it contains is extremely valuable, is well laid out, cleanly printed and easy to read. A rare combination.

Its fifteen chapters cover the creation of all types of publication from when they are merely a twinkle in the eye of the DTPer to the delivery of the final product. All the techniques you see around in the printed medium everyday are shown here. The way type works, the basics of graphic design and using visuals effectively are covered early on.

One extremely useful section cover the twenty-five most common pitfalls awaiting the novice (and even experienced) DTP user. It then goes on to show you many different layouts used to design newsletters, papers, magazines, adverts, marketing materials, books and training resources.

The last few chapters cover the way you would present the 'right image', especially in the business field and designing questionnaires and surveys. The appendices discuss colour production and technologies used.

The sub-title of this book is 'A Guide to Basic Design for Desktop Publishing' but most DTP users would give their right to come halfway close to this standard. It is an excellent book that is usable by both novices and professionals and is obviously thoroughly researched.

'Looking Good . . .' can also be used as a reference book. However, if you need a crash course in DTP design, this is the book for you. Find a quiet room for a weekend.

Author	:	Roger C. Parker
Published	:	Ventana Press
Price	:	Around £22

C. Rules of Layout

C1. The Rough Guide to Rules

In a sense, it is wrong to talk of 'rules' just as it is to say that the English language has rules. In reality, there are no rules and no right or wrong.

Style v. Fashion

By rules, designers are talking about means of expression that work for the majority of people and remain consistent over long periods of time. Women's clothes demonstrate this. Some dresses would best be described as fashionable, i.e., they are the flavour of the month. Other dresses such as the long, black cocktail dress are stylish, i.e., they never lose that appeal no matter how fashions change. Style changes very slowly.

The same is true of buildings. Soaring towers of glass, steel and concrete may have been all the rage in the Sixties and Seventies but their appeal has waned ever since. Classical architecture, however, dates back two to three thousand years and is still held as an ideal.

Focus on the Audience

In publishing, there are different rules for different situations. If you were advertising an up-market product or service then bold and eye-catching designs are out. Subtlety and sophistication are in. Often such publications can seem sparse but they work for that reason. Acres of space on a page do not detract from the object itself.

If, on the other hand, you wanted to advertise the latest craze item from the States then you would go out of your way to appeal to a section that is attracted by the latest, greatest and brightest things.

The Most Important Points

You should, first off, decide what are the most important points you have to make. This is as true of the advertising flyer as it is of the newsletter. With the former, you need to decide whether price, quality, size etc., etc., is most important and which features follow. You must rank their importance. With the newsletter you should decide which items go on the front (and to a lesser extent) the back pages. This will give you a better focus for your design and text.

Getting the Size Right

This refers to the extent of the document; should it be one side or twenty pages long. If you want something low-cost to act as a sales promotion item then this will be totally different in scale from a company's internal newspaper. Think about your potential audience, their attention span, what their situation is when reading your publication, are they busy or have time on their hands.

Information overload is a real danger in the modern world as we are bombarded on all sides by knowledge and sales pitches so that people don't always know which way to turn. Keep things to a minimum. Text should be long enough to explain the meaning but not bore the pants off the readership.

Sketch Pads

This has been mentioned before, keep a pad handy so that you can sketch pages first. This will save a lot of time and wasted effort as you should be able to spot obvious problems quite quickly and avoid them.

Navigating the Document

The eye tends to follow a line that does not run left-right, top-bottom if you use graphics and break this standard' format up. What you find is that the eye first goes to the most 'attracting' item first and then follows a line from there to the other attracting items.

The classic example is the bikini-clad girl over the bonnet of a car. Both men and women look at the girl first and then the car and then the background. Similarly, people flick the pages of a magazine and if one page has a person on it (unlike the others) then they will pause on the page longer. People are attracted to pictures of other people, the only real exception being repeated mugshots. These should be used sparingly and caringly.

The Power Balance

Basically, this means that once you have decided the order of the most important items, these should attract the eye in that order. The best example is the newspaper's headlines which splash the main story banner large and bold and the size and weight diminish with the importance of the piece.

213

Subtlety v. Hitting Them Between the Eyes

The DTPer must always be conscious of the fact that what may be technically clever may also be less than subtle and effectively detract from the desired result. The 'strength' of a document must be judged correctly. After all, upmarket products are never give gaudy banners.

Photographic Rules

When choosing photographs, make sure they are the most appropriate you can find. An article discussing geraniums will not be impressive if photos of just any old plant are used alongside. Used 'people' pictures regularly and read a good photographic magazine or book to give you the general rules of 'good' pictures.

Try to find portrait that do not suffer from 'red-eye' which is light bouncing back from the pupils when flash is used. Make sure that landscape photos are not more sky than land and that the contrast between light and dark areas is neither too great or too small. Neither will scan nor reproduce very well.

There are a whole host of supposed rules but one of the most important is that the centre of attention in the picture is large enough to be seen properly. A dot of the horizon is no use to anyone, no matter how good their eyesight.

Consistency

Most publications such as newsletters and newspapers succeed because they have found a formula that works and then applied it across the whole of the document. The sections may have different names and thrusts but there will usually be plenty of similarities between them

C2. Making and Breaking Rules

Once you have learnt all the supposed rules, you should be ready to start breaking them. The best way to do this is simply to experiment using dummy text and graphics.

Having established a style and layout that you like, show it to friends and relatives and ask for their honest opinions and to point out what they feel is right and wrong. In the light of this, go back and modify the layout based on the criticisms that you feel are justified. There is nothing like the 'acid test' of other peoples' opinions.

C3. *Good Authoring*

If you are going to be writing a lot of text, there are a few simple rules worth bearing in mind if you want to make everything much more readable.

1. Aim for your audience's level.

2. Abbreviate within text e.g., British Telecom (BT).

3. Use less than 16 words to a sentence.

4. Use **Bold** and *Italic* rather than <u>Underline</u>

5. Use 'Plain' English - Be direct and simple.

6. Break complex paragraphs down.

7. Use bullet-point or letters (a.,b.,c.,etc.) if necessary.

Index

Symbols

80286   4
80386   4
80486   4
8086   4

A

Accent   26
Adding Another Frame   171
Adding Headlines   188
Adding in Graphics   172
Adding Text   104
Adding the Text   191
Adding the Text Frames   186
Advertising Flyer   164
Advice   73
After-Sales Service   67
Align   153
Align Tool   42
Aligning   26, 137
Alignment   57, 103
Alternatives   61
Append   154
Apple Macintosh   50
Artistic   54
Artistic Text   152
AT   4
Attributes   26
Audience   212
audience   53
Auto Import   143

B

Back   58
Banner   168, 182
Baseline   26
Bitmaps   27
Blackletter   26
Block   54

Bold   26
Books   208
Bottom Line   11
box   186
Box Tool   40
Boxes   26, 128
Bring To Front   26
Brochures   208
Bubble-Jet   15, 70, 77
bubble-jet   52
Bullets   27
Business   55

C

C. P. U.   15
Carriage Return   57
Centred Text   103
Changing the Entire Font   111
Character Sets   15
Character Spacing   27, 118
charts   54
Choosing a Printer   203
Circles   129
Clear   15
Clicking   15
Clip Art   27, 172
clock speed)   4
Coffee Factor   4
Colour   72, 78
Colours   16
Columns   57
Components   73
Connections   200
Copier   202
Copy   16
Copying   140
crashed   5
Creating a Custom Page   98
Creating a Frame   100
Creating a New Page   188

Crop Image   147
Crop Marks   27
Cropping   27
Curve Down   46, 158
Curve Up   46, 158
Curves   28
Custom Page   98
Customising   45
Customising Characters   44
Customising the Screen Area   45
Cutting   16, 28, 138

D

D. T. P.   17
D.O.S.   16
Daisy-Wheel   16
databases   54
Defaults   17
Delete   17
Deleting Text   104
Deletion   28
DesignIdeas   206
Determining The Current
      Font   108
Dialog   17, 95
Dialog Box   12
Directories   17
Disk Cache Card   76
Disk Operating System   16
Display Settings   17
Distortion   155, 159
Distortion Tool   47
Distortions   28
Dividing lines   184
Dividing the Page   184
Dos   Version   82
Dos Version   81
Dot Matrix   18
Dot-Matrix   70, 77
Double-Clicking   12
Doubler Chips   75
DR Dos v6.0   82
Draft   202
Dragging   18

Drawing   131
Drawing the Text Frames   189
Drawn   54
Driver   18
Dropping   18
DTP   51
Dummy Text   170, 175
Duplicating   28, 140

E

Edit Bit Image   148
Edit Menu   43, 48
Editing   28
Editing Pictures   145
Editing Text   104
Ellipse   172
Ellipse Tool   41
Ellipses   129
Embedding   173
Entering Text   100
Entering the Text into the
      Frames   191
Equate   153
Equate Tool   42
Equating   28, 137
ESDI   68
Exporting   162, 169
Extensions   18

F

Fashion   212
File   22
File Menu   43, 47
Filenames   18
Fill   153
fill   153
Filled   143
Filled Box   136
Fills   28, 58, 130
fills   54
Final Output   202
Final Production Considera-
      tions   198
Flipping   145

Index

Flippping   29
Floppy   67, 75
Floppy Disk   19
Flowing Text Between
      Frames   174
Fonts   29, 56, 108
Fonts Supported   202
Footer   182
Footers   29
Formats   19, 144
Formatting the Text   170
Frame   171
Frame Handles   102
Frames   29
freehand   54
Front   58
Function Key   45

G

G. U. I.   19
Graphic   172
Graphics   133
Grid   29, 133
Grids   57
Grouping   19
Guidance   45
Guides   57

H

Handles   102
Hard Disk   19, 80, 81
Hard Disk Capacity   5
Hard Disks   67, 75
Hardware   20
Header   29
Headlines   30, 188
headlines   6
Help Menu   45, 47
Hidden   143
High and Low Resolutions   201
Highlighted Text   104
hung   5
Hyphenation   30, 57, 115

I

Icons   39, 46, 93
IDE   68
Image   58
Image Control   58
Image-Handling   64
Image-Setter   30
Import   143
Importing   20
Importing Pictures and Graph-
      ics   144
Indents   57
Informative   54
Ink-Jet   20, 70
Internal Memory   68
Issues   200
Italics   30

J

Justification   30, 103
Justified Text   103
Justifying Text   112

K

Kerning   31, 56, 119
Keyboard Shortcuts   48

L

Landscape   31
Laser   70, 77
Laser Printer   20
Layering   135
Layout   212
Leading   31, 56
Leaflets   208
Left-Clicking   12
Legal Rights   74
Letter-Spacing   31
Line   161
Line Spacing   120
Line Tool   41, 47
Lines   31, 58
lines   54

219

Link Tool   41
Linking   31, 105, 174
Linking the Text Frames   191
Loading an Existing Document   98
Locked   143
Logo   31, 189
logos   6
Lower-Case   31

M

Magazines   206
Manipulating Graphics   133
Manipulating Images   44
Manipulating Objects   43
Margins   32
Marks   32
megabytes   5
Memory   76, 80, 81
Memory Handling   6
Memory Size   5
Menu   20
Menus   43, 47, 93, 153
Message   95
MFM   68
Microsoft   6
Minimum   80
Monitor   20, 78
Monochrome   72, 78
MotherBoard   75
Mouse   21, 80
Move Mouse   12
Moving   134
Moving Around Documents   44
Moving the Frame   102
Moving with the Cursor Keys   101
Moving with the Mouse   101

N

Narrative   54
Navigating the Document   213
New in v2.0   84
Newspapers   207

O

Object   32
Object Specification   32
Objects   21, 130
Objects Menu   44, 48
Open   21
Options Menu   45
OverDrive   75
Overlapping   32

P

P. C.   21
Page Menu   44
Paint Program   21
Palette   24
Paragraph   57
Paragraph Spacing   32, 121
Paragraph Styles   57
Paragraph Text Styles   122
Parallel Port   22
Pasting   22, 33, 138
PC-compatible   4
Personal Use   55
photocopiers   61
Picas   33
Placing Graphics   173
Point   33
Pointer   39, 153
Pointer Tool   39
Pointers   93
Polygon Tool   46
Polygons   33, 157
Pop-Up programs   6
Port   22
Portrait   33
Ports   67
Positioning   172
PostScript   33, 71, 77
Power Balance   213
Preparation   86
presentation   54
Presets   33
Press   11
presses   50

prices   63
Printable   142
Printer   70, 77, 81, 82, 200
Printer Connections   200
Printer Margins   202
Printer Speed   201
Printing   43
Printing Options   203
Problems   89
Processor   4, 22, 66, 75, 80, 81
Proof-Reading   34
Proofs   34
Proportional   34
Punctuation Marks   34

Q

Quality   62
Queries   89

R

R.A.M.   22
R.O.M.   22
RAM   68
Random Access Memory   68
Refresh   95
Removing Dummy Text   175
Removing Excess Lines   175
Resizing   102, 134
Resolutions   201
Retrieving   43
Reversed Colours   34
Reversed-Out   34
Reversing Colours   148
Right-Aligned Text   103
Rotate   35, 160
Rotate Object   154
Rotate Tool   47
Rotating   145
Rough Guide to Rules   212
Rounded Box Tool   40
Rounded Boxes   128
Rulers   57, 94
Rules of Layout   212

S

S-VGA   78
Sans Serif   35
Saving   22
Saving as a Picture   149
Scaling   35
Scanned   54
Scanner   23
scanner   63
scanners   54
Screen   39, 71, 78, 80, 81, 92
Screen Controller Card   72
Scroll Bars   23, 94
SCSI   68
Sections   188
Select Source Text Frame   106
Selectable   142
Selecting   23, 134
Selecting Text   109
Self-Publishing   55
Send To Back   35
Separations   35
Serif   35
Set Fill Tool   41
Set Line   153
Set Line Tool   41
Setting Lines   131
Setup   85
shadow   153
Shape Toolbox   128
Shapes   58
Shaping   134
Shaping the Frame   102
Shortcuts   48, 95
Shuffle   36
Shuffled Down   136
Simms   69
Single In-line Memory Modules   69
Single In-line Plug-in   69
Size of Hard Disk   68
Size of Screen   72, 78
Sizes   56
Sizing   172, 173
Sketch Pads   213

Slots 67
Snap To Grid 36
Software 23
Solid 36
Solid Pictures 147
Specifications 142
Speech Marks 36
Speed 4, 62
spreadsheets 54
Stacking 36, 135
Standard Layouts 96
Starting the Program 92
Statement 12
Stories 36
Storing 43
Story Flow 105
Style 212
Styles 36
Subhead 37
Super-VGA 72
System Unit 23

T

T.S.R. 6
tables 54
Tabs 57
Tabulation 37, 57, 112
Technical Support 89
Template 97
Templates 37
Terminate and Stay Resident 6
Text 153
Text Formatting 112
Text and Dialog Keys 45
Text Distortion 155
Text Editors 63
Text Formatting 103
Text Frame Margins 115
Text Frame Tool 40
Text
    Frames 100, 174, 186, 189, 191
Text Input Dialog Box 155
Text Manipulation Tools 155
Text Menu 44, 48

Text Tool 39
Text Wrap 172
Text Wrap Tool 42
Text-Handling 64
Text-Processors 63
TextEf-
    fect 6, 42, 46, 152, 168, 189
TextEffect Screen 46
Thumb 94
Tilde 37
Titles 37
ToolBox 153
Toolbox 24
Top of Caps 37
Tracking 37, 56
Transparent 37, 58, 147
Type 12
Type Attributes 110
Type Face 109
Type Sizes 110
Type Styles 56
Typeface 38
Typefaces 56

U

Umlaut 38
Undo 24
Units 38
Unlink Tool 42
Unlinking 38, 105
Upgradeable Chips 66
Upgrading 75, 83
UPPER-CASE 38

V

VGA 72, 78
View 24

W

W.I.M.P. 25
W.Y.S.I.W.Y.G 25
Warranties 78
Windows 88
wissywig 25

Word-Processor   63
Wrap Around   143
Wrapping Text   38, 170
Wraps   58

X

XT   4

Z

Zooming   25
Zooming In   107
Zooming Out   107

Dedications

To Rosie for all the tea and sympathy throughout the hard slog

To Steve White for his editing and proofing talents